The
Design
of
Books

The
Design
of
Books

An Explainer *for* Authors, Editors, Agents, *and* Other Curious Readers

Debbie Berne

THE UNIVERSITY OF CHICAGO PRESS

Chicago and London

The University of Chicago Press, Chicago 60637
The University of Chicago Press, Ltd., London
© 2024 by Deborah Berne

Published 2024
Printed in the United States of America

33 32 31 30 29 28 27 26 25 24   2 3 4 5

ISBN-13: 978-0-226-82295-2 (paper)
ISBN-13: 978-0-226-83266-1 (ebook)
DOI: https://doi.org/10.7208/chicago/9780226832661.001.0001

Library of Congress Cataloging-in-Publication Data
Names: Berne, Debbie, author.
Title: The design of books : an explainer for authors, editors, agents,
    and other curious readers / Debbie Berne.
Other titles: Chicago guides to writing, editing, and publishing.
Description: Chicago : The University of Chicago Press, 2024. |
    Series: Chicago guides to writing, editing, and publishing |
    Includes bibliographical references and index.
Identifiers: LCCN 2023033202 | ISBN 9780226822952 (paperback) |
    ISBN 9780226832661 (ebook)
Subjects: LCSH: Book design. | Publishers and publishing.
Classification: LCC Z246 .B475 2024 | DDC 744.5/2—dc23/eng20231011
LC record available at https://lccn.loc.gov/2023033202

To Caroline Herter,
who taught me to *see* books

Contents

Introduction

Congratulations, you wrote a book! Well, not exactly. That document you've been living with for months, or more likely years, writing and revising, nurturing and cursing, isn't a book yet—it's a manuscript. And, sorry, no one wants to read your Word doc, no matter how beautifully written it is. It's not a book unless it's designed to be a book.

That digital file becomes an object people leave out on their coffee tables or snuggle up with on the couch through publishing. *Publish* means "to make public" and can involve an author uploading a file to a website and making every decision about it while sitting alone at their kitchen table. Or it can mean months of back-and-forth with a team of professionals at a publishing house, with many interests and voices shaping the final product. Whatever the path to print (or ebook; we'll get to that), at some point that digital file will be stamped "final" and given over to a designer, an art director, a compositor, or formatting software. The text will get a trim size, a typeface, a cover design. Eventually, ink will hit paper, pages will be bound together, and that familiar, beloved, three-dimensional object will emerge.

The first transfer of a Word doc into a design file is called a pour. Designers pour words into their layout files like hot metal into a mold. A text can take on a thousand different shapes. An edition of *Moby-Dick* might be three hundred or five hundred pages long depending on the size of the page, the type, and the margins. It could be a thick brick of a paperback with small, tightly set type and a flimsy paper cover or a large, cloth-bound hardcover with fields of white space, color illustrations, and gold stamping along the page edges. The text doesn't change, of course; every copy begins "Call me Ishmael." But there are infinite possibilities for look and feel, each with its own vibe.

Most people—including most authors—don't know much about book design. You may not even be fully aware that books, aside from their covers, *are* designed. Because books are so common and the layout of a page so familiar, it doesn't occur to many readers that someone is thinking about details like where the page number should go or how wide the margins should be—or that these decisions make any difference whatsoever. They do. You may not consider the size of a book or its format—hardcover, paperback—to be aspects of its design, but they are.

Design encompasses all the elements of the object from the choice of typeface to the choice of paper. Effective design makes books appealing and useful. An interesting cover beckons readers—"Ooh, what's that?"—and lets them know what a book is about and what it's like. Design inside a book creates order and bestows authority (warranted or not). Confident use of typography, hierarchy, and space guides readers, showing them where to look and how to make their way. Reading a badly designed book is like driving over a crumbling road, potholes everywhere.

• • •

As a freelance book designer, I've designed hundreds of books over the last twenty years. I work for big publishing houses and small ones, independent editors, authors who are self-publishing, and, on occasion, agents. I've designed cookbooks and kids' books, business, gardening, mindfulness, art, craft, gift, and reference books, YA, fiction, and poetry. There's a wonderful panoply of books out there, each one doing its own special thing.

I wrote this book as a guide to help authors better understand how design works in and for *their* books. When a professional writer I know told me she didn't know the trim size of her own book until it arrived—when it showed up, printed and bound, she realized she had bought the wrong size envelopes to send out complimentary copies—I was reminded of how estranged writers can be from the production of their own work. Many authors haven't considered design at all when writing and developing their books and then don't know what they're looking at or how to engage. Or they *have* fantasized about how their book will look but don't know how to talk about it.

Editors, agents, and other publishing professionals are generally familiar with the stages of the design process, but they may not think it has much to do with them. For instance, there's often a lot of conversation around the literary (and literal) meaning of titles without much consideration of their visual impact. On a book cover, short words act differently than long words—they can be set larger, they look better stacked, they are often more legible in all caps. I'm not suggesting that everyone's titles be made up of only short words, but it is helpful to think through how titles and subtitles will function graphically—that is, what the words look like—while you're still thinking through what those words will be. Some folks on the editorial (or sales and marketing) side are tuned in to how design interacts with editorial structure and language. Others, less so. I'm always hoping for more cross-pollination. Design and editorial concerns go hand in hand; more input from (and understanding of) the design side will help everyone on the publishing team work smarter and, ultimately, produce better books.

•••

In the chapters that follow I explain all the things I wish the writers and editors I work with knew about book design. I walk through the anatomy of a book—what all the parts are and how they fit together. I describe the printer's specifications: the choices about size, binding, paper, and printing that have a major impact on how a book ultimately looks and feels. Then I delve into typography, how books are traditionally organized and sequenced, the classic book page and why it looks that way, what typesetting is and why it matters. Both illustrated books and ebooks have their own particularities and get their own chapters. Of course, we'll talk covers. If that's why you're here, flip directly to chapter 3.

The final chapter is about the design process and specifically centers the author. If your book is your baby, the publishing process can feel a bit like a kidnapping. The design piece, for those working with a publishing house, can feel strangely fraught—so foundational and yet out of your hands, seeming to take place behind a velvet rope with an intimidating bouncer standing guard. I hope understanding the stages your text will pass through on its way to the printer (or the Kindle store) will bring some orientation. Authors who are self-publishing have a lot to manage, and I walk through the basics of finding and working with a professional designer (for a cover at the very least) and discuss some basic guardrails for formatting book interiors should you decide to take that on.

Throughout the book I explain best practices for book design. Of course, my own preferences and particular ways of working inevitably soak through. There's no question that other designers feel differently about the use of bold italic (and many other things) than I do. Different kinds of books require different solutions, individual designers have their own ways of doing things, and questions of aesthetics are always up for discussion. But it's not a free-for-all. The principles that undergird book design are there for a reason—to create clarity and sense on the page; to make reading effortless; to allow the ideas of the author to shine. What those principles are, and why they work, is what we are about to explore.

Design isn't (only) about making things look pretty. It's structural, like the beams supporting a building. It's navigational, like the signs that guide you at the airport. And it impacts meaning. The choice of font, to take just one example, tells the reader something, whether they're aware of the cues or not (and they almost always aren't). This is true for covers and interiors, printed books and digital ones. *This* book is an introduction to book design and an invitation to consider it more integrally in the development of your projects. I hope you come away with a better sense of what book design does and how to speak its language. (Design, like most crafts, is full of jargon. See the glossary at the end of this book for quick reference.) Once you have names for all the parts and pieces of book and page, you'll never look at a part title, running head, or endpaper the same way. These elements aren't fixed but choices to be made, every time.

Welcome to the hidden world of book design, word people!

Chapter 1
The Physical Book

When ebooks emerged in the early '00s, no one worried that writing was going to disappear. We know we'll always have people who write things and others who want to read them. It was the book as a physical object that was threatened. In contrast to the paperless, weightless ebook, the printed book, which had always seemed so handy—just tuck it in your bag and go—was seen as expensive, environmentally unsound, a pain to procure, and rather cumbersome. But while ebooks and audiobooks have earned their place in the market and the internet serves forth plenty of great writing every day, printed books have persisted, and even thrived, in the digital era. The design writer Caroline Roberts observed, "In an increasingly disposable world, books represent permanence and continuity. The tactile quality of books is a joy that should not be underestimated. It is what will ensure their longevity."[1]

Design and production choices are what distinguish beautiful books from mediocre ones and average-looking books from ugly ones. Decisions regarding size, paper, kind of cover, and printing are aesthetic and expressive choices—as well as economic ones, to be sure—that are integral to a book's look and feel. Because production and materials make up a substantial part of a book's budget, they're usually determined early on as part of the financial equation of acquiring a title. While publishers want their books to look and feel good, they may compromise on certain aspects of production to make the numbers work. Design input at this stage is useful. Designers are good at envisioning a manuscript (or book idea) as the specific physical object it is going to become. Does a standard size and treatment make the most sense? Would something distinctive in the package add value (and what might that be)? Which compromises are tolerable? What could we do to offset the ones that are not? Publishers don't reinvent the wheel with every book. Many books work beautifully in standard sizes with standard paper and printing and are affordable to produce only when slotted into existing formats.

Authors working with traditional publishers should be aware of the decisions being made around their books. Is your book going to be hardcover or paperback (or eventually both) and at what size? Will there be a jacket? What will the paper look and feel like? If you're producing a book yourself, don't just click through the options offered by the printer or service provider. Think about what you want the final package to look like. The look and feel of the paper is key to a good reading experience. Printers will usually send examples of their various papers and cover stocks by request.

No matter your scenario, to understand the conversation around design and production issues you need a grasp of the basics—how books are made, what choices are available, and what those choices communicate to readers. I can't emphasize enough how crucial these fundamental early decisions are to a book's success in the market and its abiding satisfaction as an object.

Kinds of Books

A book lets you know how to interact with it. You might prop a cookbook on the kitchen counter, reading it standing up with one eye on the text and the other on the electric mixer. When reading with a child, you might sit in an armchair with a picture book spread over both your laps. I love to read novels curled on the couch, one hand spreading the pages, the other deep in a bowl of popcorn. But you can't comfortably curl up with the popcorn bowl and, say, an atlas. A small paperback tucks into your purse but won't read well, or stay put, propped on the counter. Readers know how different kinds of books should look and feel—their size, weight, orientation, and bulk; what publishing folks call their format.

There are many variables that determine how a book fits into the literary landscape—is it fiction or nonfiction, adult or children's, academic or trade? The kind of book it is determines how it's conceived and written, edited, pitched, priced, printed, published, and read. Different kinds of books require different packages and different editorial approaches and take significantly different amounts of time and creativity to design. This question, "What kind of book is it?" comes up again and again in the chapters that follow.

For now, let's consider a fundamental distinction designers make: Is a book illustrated or text only? The term *illustrated book* refers to books that feature images—be they photographs, drawings, paintings, or art in any other medium. This category includes children's picture books, cookbooks, travel guides and field guides, how-to and reference books (art, craft, gardening, mechanics, etc.), art books, design and lifestyle books, graphic novels, comic anthologies, and illustrated fiction. These books might be flipped through or read selectively— rather than straight through—and returned to again and again.

The presence of illustrations drives many design decisions. While most books are vertically oriented (portrait), an illustrated book might be square or horizontal (landscape) if it is meant to sit across a lap, or two, or if that proportion better suits the images. It might be oversized, requiring two hands or to be laid on a table to be enjoyed. Some illustrated books are thought of as "coffee-table books" (designers don't use this term). While this may suggest an (outdated) assumption about the prevalence of coffee tables and what they should be used for, it also speaks to the size, heft, and status of many illustrated books. We not only read (or look at) them, but they become part of our decor, an expression of taste and identity. Their design is often an explicit aspect of their appeal.

Text-driven or text-only books—which are most books—are usually intended for extended reading and are designed with this in mind. They're printed in black ink (almost always) on paper that isn't too heavy or too starkly white, so they are portable and easy on the eyes. Hardcovers tend to run around 6 × 9 inches, just on the edge of what is comfortable to hold in one hand. Paperbacks are often a little smaller, and therefore easier to hold. I've always loved the pocket book (or mass-market) size for how easy it is to carry around, sometimes literally in my back pocket, and to hold when reading. Books are almost never smaller than 4 × 6 inches (about the size of a postcard) or they will quite literally get lost on the shelf.

The most successful books might be published as a hardcover first, then later as a trade paperback, and finally sometimes in mass-market size. Each incarnation has a different sensibility, even when they share identical cover design. The size, proportion, and length of a book are often the very first things a reader takes note of (when browsing in a bookstore, at least—the inability to make those quick evaluations is one of the inadequacies of online book shopping). A book's format is expressive.

The Parts of a Book

The kind of books we all read—pieces of paper stacked on top of each other and bound together on one side—is called a codex.[2] The name comes from the Latin word *caudex*, meaning "the trunk of a tree, wooden tablet, or book." It is the latest and most successful book construction, a category that also includes clay tablets and scrolls. (Tablets, the earliest form of the book, have finally circled back as a popular format in the form of e-readers.) A codex is handy, sturdy, and easy to use. It allows for random access—you can open it to any part—in contrast to scrolls, which must be unwound and sifted through sequentially.[3] Pages can be printed on both sides, creating efficiency in their manufacture and their use.

As familiar as books are, and as often as most of us have handled them, most people don't know what the parts of a book are called or how they function. What's to know? Books work so well that there's rarely a need to consider their mechanics (unlike my laptop, my phone, and my electric toothbrush, which I'm always cursing). But part of a book's design is the way that it's put together, so here's a primer on its anatomy. If you pull a book off the shelf and have it nearby as you read through this section, it will help you identify and make sense of the terms and descriptions that follow.

The Anatomy of a Hardcover

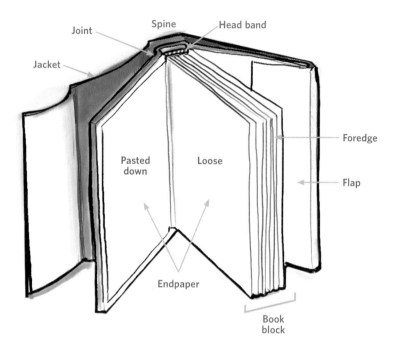

The Jacket

The jacket, also known as the dustjacket, is a paper wrapper usually around a hardcover book. (Paperbacks can have jackets too, and it's not uncommon for books for the European market, but in the US it's a rarity.) For hundreds of years books didn't have covers, as they weren't even sold bound. The book buyer had to make that happen for themselves. Imagine! It wasn't until the nineteenth century that publishers started machine-binding each book in cloth or leather and wrapping it in a disposable paper jacket to protect the more beautiful case beneath. Times change, and these days jackets are usually the star of the show. (Even so, in my household jackets are regarded as "annoying" and are flung off as soon as we're back from the bookstore.)

Jackets are standard practice for most new hardcover books, although there is some shift away from them, particularly for kids' books, young adult fiction, and cookbooks—some of the most design-forward genres. The presence of a jacket can create a certain image for a book—important, elegant, serious—while the lack of one might make it feel hip and more casual. On the other hand, a jacket with a high-energy, wraparound design can be exciting and modern, while a stamped cloth-bound book will feel traditional, or timeless. I will talk more about the design of jackets in chapter 3.

The Case

The hard cover of a hardcover book is called its case, and hardcover books are properly called casebound. The case is made of two boards—front and back—which are covered in a paper or cloth wrapper (the casewrap) that holds it all together. (There is also a three-piece case where a third board is inserted behind the spine.[4]) Take out a hardcover book and remove the jacket—you're looking at the case. When you open the book wide, notice the little pocket of space between the flexible book block and the spine. This construction lets the book lie nice and flat on a table.

In a book with a jacket, the case is hidden and readers may never pull back the flaps to give it a look. Regardless, it must be designed. The designer, or sometimes the editor or art director (the primary contact between design and editorial, see page 170 for more on that role), will choose a solid color paper or cloth for the casewrap (these days it's almost always a faux cloth, which is more readily available and more economical than linen or cotton) that complements the jacket and endpapers.

The front and back covers of the case will often be left blank, with the book's title, author's name, and publisher's logo stamped along the spine so that even if the jacket is lost, it will still be clear what book it is (although you probably won't be able to resell it at the used bookstore). For children's books, designers will often repeat the full jacket design identically on the case, wisely suspecting that kids might toss or otherwise damage jackets. On occasion, a request by the designer (or author) and a willingness by the publisher will result in a little extra design on the front of the casewrap. This could be the book's title, the author's initials (it's oddly common), a relevant illustration, or a decorative ornament. These front cover designs don't really serve any function (although they do indicate the front side of the book). Rather, they're secret delights, left there for the reader who bothers to unwrap the book and discover them.

For books without a jacket—on cookbooks, for instance, a jacket is just a nuisance—the cover design lives directly on the case. Cases can be printed, just like any paper cover, but they're often stamped instead. Stamping is a process where the design is pressed into the paper (or cloth) and the board behind it with a die. This depression can be left blank (this is blindstamping) or filled with pigment or colored foil. Stamping can look cool—dimensional, analog, and tactile—but has its limitations, allowing for only a very limited number of colors (three would be a lot). Typography and line illustration take well to stamping. If the case design uses a photograph or a watercolor, it will need to be printed. Sometimes printing and stamping are used together on a cover.

The Spine

The spine is the part of a book that's visible when it's sitting on the shelf. It holds and supports a book's pages. For hardcovers, the spine can be rounded, which is traditional, or flat, for which an additional, narrow board is inserted. For paperbacks, the paper cover is scored and folded to create the spine. A spine's width will increase or decrease depending on the length of the book. A book with very few pages, like a children's picture book, will have a very thin spine, maybe only a quarter of an inch—such a little bit of room for type. Whether on a jacket, case, or paperback, spines almost always display the author's name (often just their last name—easier for alphabetizing), the title (but usually not the subtitle), and the publisher's logo. Designing for the spine is a pleasure of book design. More on that in chapter 3.

The Joint, or Hinge

Look again at the case of your book and notice the groove along the front and back covers close to the spine. This is called the joint or the hinge (interchangeably), which allows the covers to swing open and closed like a door. This may seem a small detail to you, but it's not to the designer—there's a ditch running down the front (and back) cover of the book. If there's a jacket, the joint will be hidden, but if there's no jacket, it will be visible as part of the cover design. I like a jacketless book, but reckoning with that ditch is no joke. Without careful attention, important elements of the cover can fall into the joint, distorting or swallowing them, or a centered design can appear off-center. Heartbreak.

Endpapers

Endpapers are the strong sheets of paper at the front and back that hold the inside and the outside (the book block and the case) of a hardcover book together. One side is pasted down against the cover and the other is attached to the book block (the loose page is called the flyleaf). These anchors let a book's pages sit within the case but also rise away from the spine to allow the book to fall open. They're almost always a heavy, uncoated sheet, regardless of what paper is used within. Paperbacks don't use or need endpapers.

In text-only books, endpapers often match the text stock and are barely distinguishable from the rest of the book. For illustrated and other design-focused books, endpapers can be a design element— printed with solid colors, maps, decorative patterns, or reference information. Antiquarian books, and books that are trying to look like antiquarian books, sometimes use marbled paper for their endsheets. In kids' picture books, endpapers are used in all sorts of whimsical ways (Mo Willems is a master of the clever endpaper). In a book without a jacket, the copy that would have gone on the flaps—sales copy and the author bio—can be printed on the endpapers instead.

Head and Tail Bands

Head and tail (H&T) bands are the funny little worms that live at the top and bottom of the book, along the spine. It's possible you've never noticed them, but look again at your hardcover book—there they are! Originally H&T bands were sewn in to reinforce the top of the spine, which we tug at when pulling a book off the shelf.[5] As binding techniques evolved, H&T bands were no longer needed for reinforcement but survived as a decorative detail. They come in a rainbow of options and also in striped and checkerboard patterns.

The Paper Cover

The terms I've covered so far have referred to the parts of a hardcover book. Paperback books are bound in paper rather than a case made of boards. The paperback cover is one piece of heavy paper, scored to turn at the spine, and trimmed along with the book block, making the cover and the pages exactly the same size. The book block is (usually) pasted directly into the spine, so it doesn't separate from the body of the book when you open it. If a book is bound tightly, the spine will need to be "cracked" so it can open fully. Some paperbacks have a scored hinge which acts a little like the joint on a hardcover—helping the cover fold back and providing a little extra support to the book block.

The Book Block

The "inside" of a book is a bound set of pages called the book block. Books are traditionally printed on large sheets of paper, thirty-two, sixteen, or eight pages to a side. The sheet is then folded and folded and folded again until it's a tidy booklet called a signature. A finished book is made up of many signatures—gathered and bound together— so the final page count will end up a multiple of eight. If your text ends on page 93, you'll be left with three blank pages at the end: ninety-three pages isn't a possible page count, but ninety-six is. Most readers won't notice those blank pages, and they're common in text-only books. In illustrated and other design-focused books, empty pages are generally avoided—designers feel it looks unpolished and will pad, stretch, and squeeze the text, trying to put something on every page. (An index is relatively easy to compress or expand and is often handy for filling pages, when available.)

Once printed, a book's pages are bound together by either thread or glue and then trimmed. Sewn bindings are traditional and durable. You can see if a book is sewn by cracking it open near the center—the

A Sixteen-Page Signature

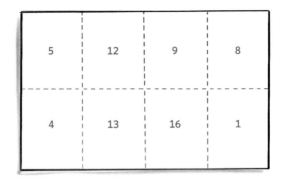

Book pages are printed flat on a large sheet, eight pages per side,

then folded,

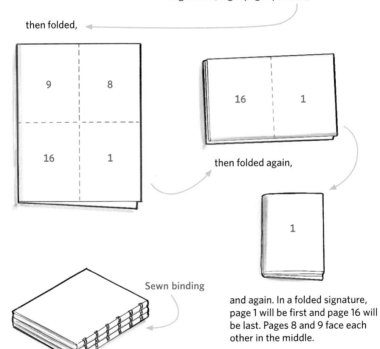

then folded again,

and again. In a folded signature, page 1 will be first and page 16 will be last. Pages 8 and 9 face each other in the middle.

Sewn binding

Folded signatures are gathered in sequence and, when bound together, form the book block.

long stitches should be visible in the gutter. Using glue is cheaper than sewing, and most paperbacks (and, increasingly, many hardcover books) are glued—most commonly perfect bound. While surely not as elegant, glued bindings have come a long way. They now can match sewn bindings in terms of sturdiness; the days of pages falling out of a book as you read are mostly over. Glued bindings will never lie completely flat, but remember this matters only for certain kinds of books. You don't generally need your copy of *Gone Girl* to lie flat.

Printer's Specifications

A book is a manufactured object and the methods and materials used to create it can vary widely. Next time you're at the bookstore, check out the books with your hands as well as your eyes (or try this on your own bookshelf). Notice the different sizes and proportions, paperbacks versus hardcovers, jackets versus jacketless covers, different tones and thicknesses of papers (both inside the book and for the cover or jacket), rounded versus square spines, flashy foils and stamping. Although books all have the same basic parts, it's a jumble of visual personalities on the shelf. The instructions for how a book is to be printed, bound, covered, and delivered are called the printer's (or production) specifications, or specs. The choices made for each title are based on editorial, economic, and market factors, and they're *also* design decisions that will help determine the character of an individual book. I love thinking through specs and wondering what different trim sizes or formats might communicate about a book—how it will fit in with and stand out from the others on the shelf. Since cost is such an important factor here, these choices are often made at the executive level. It's smart to involve designers in these conversations. We might just come up with something fresh that doesn't add to (or is worth) the cost. Here are the basics.

Format

Books can be bound inside boards, to make a hardcover, or in a paper cover to make a paperback. Publishers think through how they would like a book to show up in the market and choose the book's format—essentially, its package—accordingly. You are probably familiar with the convention of releasing books first as hardcovers—with their higher status and price tag—followed by a more affordable paperback, to capture a wider audience, a year or so later, and sometimes a mass-market version. Each of these marks a shift in the book's format.[6]

Paperbacks have generally been considered the poor cousin of hardcovers, which are more sturdily bound and last longer. Yes, hardcovers look nice on your bookshelf. And there's status associated with being published in hardcover. But paperbacks are more affordable, more portable, and often easier to actually read because they're smaller and lighter. Paperbacks can feel workmanlike, handy, deliberately casual, or slim and elegant. Paperbacks can have flaps. If your book is print on demand, it will most likely be a paperback. And most books meant to be read straight through are a pleasure in this format. The hegemony of hardcovers—particularly for fiction—belongs to an earlier era. The future of publishing probably looks a lot like a paperback.[7]

Trade paperback refers to paperbacks that are around the same size as most hardcover books. If a book comes out first in hardcover, then in paperback, the same interior layout can be used for both if the page size doesn't change. Another kind of paperback—and considered a separate format in publishing—is the mass-market paperback. These are the pocket-sized books (4¼ × 7 inches) that are sold in supermarkets, drug stores, and airports (as well as at bookstores), sometimes on revolving racks. Mass-market is generally reserved for genre fiction—romance, mystery, westerns, etc.—and their, often, voracious readers. Readers who go through a couple of books a week aren't looking for a beautiful object but an inexpensive and convenient one. Ebooks, even more convenient, address the same audience and have encroached on the mass-market format in the past decade.

Formats

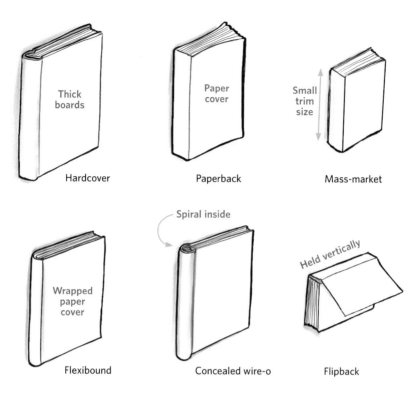

While they are much (much) less common, I'd be remiss not to mention some of the other possible formats. In my twenty-plus years as a book designer, I've designed four books with spiral bindings—referred to as a wire-o in publishing circles. They're tempting for certain kinds of books—craft and other technique-y books—because they lie *so* nice and flat. The (major) drawback: no spine. Bookstores don't want to shelve a book without a spine, and even if they did, no one would be able to figure out what book it was without pulling it all the way off the shelf and looking at its cover. Publishers have tried to remedy this situation by creating the so-called concealed wire-o (there's also a "semiconcealed" wire-o) where the spiral is hidden inside a bulbous—but printable!—spine.

There's another binding called flexibind which is bound like a hardcover but with a light, flexible cover rather than a stiff board. Flexibinding was first used for bibles, which benefit from a binding that can lie flat, like a hardcover, but aren't overly bulky. In the past couple of decades flexibinding has become popular for other kinds of (mostly illustrated) books as well.

In 2009, a Dutch publisher brought another format to market: the *dwarsligger*. About the size of a cell phone, these paperback books are constructed to be held vertically in one hand (facing pages are top and bottom rather than left and right), the pages turned with a thumb-led upswipe like flipping through your text messages. Seen as a possible next big thing—the perfect read for the subway, when one hand is busy holding the strap—the format, now coined a flipback, was launched into the US market in 2019 with Penguin Random House's repackaging of books by John Green, the author of the megaselling *The Fault in Our Stars*. I don't know how those sold, but there wasn't a tidal wave of other titles to follow. The format may have been a poor fit for the pandemic era when fewer people commuted and portability wasn't as prized. But it may break through yet. It's nice to think that people are still imagining ways to improve, or expand upon, the trusty codex.

Trim Size

Trim size is the term for the size of the book block, the size of the page. In a paperback book it will also be the size of the book itself. In a hardcover, the case will extend by ⅛ inch or so around the book block and so is a little larger than the trim size. When publishing folks talk about the size of the book, they're referring to its trim size.

Working out the right size and proportion of each title is one of the arts of publishing. Text-only trade books usually fall within a pretty narrow range of sizes, but even within those you will find books that are a little narrower or a little squatter than the rest. Publishers often slot books into a few standard sizes—6 × 9 inches (portrait, or vertical, orientation) being the most common—that use paper most efficiently and economically. But even within the range of standard sizes, there are choices available; 5½ × 8½ inches is also a standard paper size. Notice how even ½ inch more or less in either dimension affects the way a book feels.

For illustrated, reference, and gift books, there are more possibilities for size and proportion. A designer or art director (along with the editor, marketing team, production manager, and publisher) will consider the elements of the text (are there sidebars, tables, diagrams?) that might call for a larger or wider page. Books featuring photographs and full-color art need to be big enough to let the images shine, and the size of the illustrations might determine the most suitable size (and proportion) for the book. A small trim size can feel friendly, useful, or gifty and, if you're lucky, might be displayed on the counter at the bookstore. Something slender has a totally different sensibility from a square or horizontally oriented book. Aside from purely aesthetic factors, availability and efficient use of paper will help determine the best options for sizing.

Color

In publishing, color refers to the number of inks that will be used to print the inside of a book. A one-color book uses just one ink, and in the vast majority of books that one ink is black. (Covers are assumed to be four color unless otherwise specified.) You can still include images in a one-color book, but they will be "black and white"—the design term is grayscale. Shades of gray (50 percent black, for instance) can be used to add visual variety, to create hierarchy, or as a design element. For instance, a gray box behind a sidebar will differentiate it from the rest of the text (more on that in chapter 4).

A four-color book is a "full-color" book. Those four colors are cyan, magenta, yellow, and black—referred to as CMYK or process color. When combined, these four inks can create thousands of colors. If you have color photography or other colorful art in your book, it will be printed in four colors.

To my mind, the classiest book on the block is the two-color book, a term that usually refers to black ink plus one other color (although it can also be two inks, neither of which is black). The second color acts as a contrast to the black printing, highlighting certain elements and bringing a little verve to the page, as in *this* book. Some books lend themselves more readily to this kind of treatment, which is significantly more expensive than one-color printing—diagrams, tables, sidebars, or line illustrations might justify the cost of a second color. Books featuring straight text are rarely printed in two colors.

Two-color books are printed with two solid inks, rather than built up from a combination of CMYK. The most common way to do this is to use Pantone inks (there are other ink makers, but Pantone is the industry standard in the US and most likely what you will run across). You may see designers looking through Pantone swatch or chip books, which display a rainbow of colors in little rectangles, to pick a specific yellowish red or greenish blue. Solid inks produce strong, reliable color. In addition to being used in two-color printing, they can be used alongside CMYK for an extra pop. Digital printers don't use Pantone colors. If you are printing digitally, your choices are limited to CMYK or black.

Page Count

One of the biggest expenses, and headaches, of publishing is the paper. Every additional signature costs money and adds weight, making it more expensive to ship. When considering the length of a book, publishers think about how much paper they're paying for and what the shipping charges will be. That said, publishers (usually) want books to feel substantial, and the longer a book is, the more they can charge for it. Publishers weigh the production cost, retail price, length, bulk (how thick a book is), and reader expectations to determine how long they want a book to be.

You might be thinking, "Um, I thought *I* determine the length of my book by how many words I write" (or how many words have been agreed to in your contract). Not entirely. Designers can manipulate the length of a book in all sorts of ways—page size, type size, margin size, font choice, even how much space there is between each line will affect a book's page count (see chapter 4). Reducing or enlarging font size or margins to make a targeted page count isn't uncommon.

Paper

There are many book papers to choose from, and the folks on the design and production team consider their weight, color, smoothness, opacity, and feel to the touch when choosing paper for a particular book (not to mention what's available, what's affordable). Books are mostly paper, so whatever is chosen will have a big impact on a reader's experience.

Text-only books are printed on uncoated paper that is light and easy to handle. Stark white paper is hard on the eyes, and books meant for extended reading are usually printed on soft white papers, often called natural, which are warm and creamy. Illustrated books are usually printed on brighter, heavier, coated paper that is less porous—causing the ink to bleed less—so the images print sharply. Think of the difference between a newspaper (uncoated) and a magazine (coated). Coated papers come in different weights (all paper comes in different weights) and in finishes that range from glossy to dull. Matte and satin coatings are less reflective than a high gloss and often have a nicer tactile quality (more like paper, less like plastic). For books that include a lot of images and a lot of text, publishers must balance the benefits of a coated sheet for nice reproduction of images with its drawbacks: causing the words printed in black ink to reflect light, requiring the reader to tilt the pages this way and that to combat the effect.

Paper choice is a decision—usually made with little input from the editor or author—that must balance aesthetic, production, and financial factors. The availability of paper for books has become an increasingly serious issue, particularly since the COVID-19 pandemic. Fine paper, which is used for books, makes up only a fraction of the paper market in the US, and paper mills have converted their production to meet the higher demand for packaging material like corrugated boxes and other brown papers.[8] The consolidation of paper mills and the aging of their workforce are also factors limiting supply.[9] These trends have caused paper shortages, printing delays, price increases, and a lot of concern in the publishing industry. It's likely that there will be more limited paper choices in the foreseeable future, at the least with paper made in the US. Maybe shortages will drive innovation: Can

Printing a Book

Below are the aspects to consider for the manufacture of a physical book. This is not a comprehensive list—who knows what people will imagine—but it covers most of the bases. No single book will employ every element.

General
Format (paperback, hardcover, other)
Trim size
Page count
Print run
Paper stock
Printing/inks

Cover, case, or jacket
Paper stock
Printing/inks
Lamination
Spot gloss
Stamping
Embossing/debossing
Die cut
Other effects
Flaps (size)

Case only
Material
Board weight
Spine (round, square)
Head & tail bands
Endpapers

Additional elements or effects
Gatefold
Ribbon marker
Belly band or O-band
Sticker
Beveled edges
Edge staining
Slipcase

Shipping instructions

designers successfully reimagine lower-grade or brown papers for use in certain kinds of books? The challenge is out there.

Printing Effects and Other Extras

With the increasing emphasis on printed books as beauty objects, and as new technologies become available, designers see the physical aspects of a book as a place to communicate and innovate. Children's books, cookbooks, gift books, and literary fiction are all genres that tend toward high production values and the creative use of materials.

Almost all book covers are laminated to protect them from scuffing and dings. Just like house paint, this lamination can be glossy, semigloss (or satin), or matte. Glossy covers are shiny and reflective. You can wipe the food stains right off them, so they're often used for textbooks and children's books (but, ironically, more rarely for cookbooks). Matte laminations create a more subtle look—you may not notice the coating at all—and are common for books meant to be taken as serious or classy. Paperback covers should always have a lay-flat lamination, which keeps the cover from curling up.

On top of the base coat a designer can add a spot gloss, a clear reflective coating that is applied to specific areas of a cover or jacket. Lots of covers, in many genres, use spot gloss on title type or illustrations, making those areas shiny and drawing the reader's eye. If you run your finger over a cover that uses spot gloss, you can feel the smooth, raised finish.

Special inks and foils (including metallic and neon) can make a cover stand out in fun or unexpected ways. Science fiction and fantasy covers often use metallic foils to suggest spaceships or armor. Mysteries and thrillers (and other kinds of books too) sometimes use embossing, which makes titles or other cover elements literally pop out from the background. Journals and other books that readers write in or personalize may have belly bands or O-bands (bands of paper that go around a book's case) or removable stickers so that the commercial aspects of the book—sales copy, bar code—can be removed after purchase.

Other special treatments include rounded corners, ribbon markers, edge staining (often for bibles), die cuts, gatefolds, and deckled page edges. The classic children's book *The Very Hungry Caterpillar* uses both die cuts (cutting out a shape in the paper) and a gatefold (a page that opens to twice its width or more) to memorable effect. Deckled page edges were a status symbol in the seventeenth century and modern books occasionally assume this affectation. Real deckling—retaining the ragged edge of the sheet rather than trimming it off—is a headache for printers and many offer only a faux deckle in which signatures are offset to create the impression of a nonuniform foredge.

Of course, extra effects cost extra money and publishers often need to be convinced of their worth. Special effects are mostly tactile and often don't translate well to the flat, one-inch cover images many readers first encounter online. Some of the most beautifully produced books look just ho-hum on Amazon because you can't see the physical qualities that make them stand out in a bookstore. Many special effects aren't available for books printed digitally. And there are environmental costs to special effects (and to be honest, the manufacturing of all books). Coatings and laminates are plastics, shrink-wrap is unconscionably wasteful, and the glues and chemicals used in papermaking, printing, and binding can be toxic to workers and the environment. Conscientious publishers can make more environmentally responsible choices by talking with printers about the inks, papers, and other materials they use.[10]

Printing

One of the responsibilities of a traditional publisher is anticipating (and generating) interest in a title, weighing it against the costs of production and warehousing, and deciding on a suitable print run. Compared to most mass-produced items, books are printed in small quantities and sold in even smaller ones. An initial print run of five thousand copies is solid. Ten to twenty thousand means your publisher has really high hopes. Many books sell less than a thousand copies over their lifetime. How many units are printed and by what method are important factors in the equation of how much the production of a book will cost a publisher, and hence, how many pages they agree to, whether they want to print hardcover or paperback, whether you get that spot gloss on the jacket, and what the retail price will be (which will lure or repel your potential readers).

Almost all newly published commercial, or "trade," books are printed using offset lithography. Offset printing is an efficient and high-quality process that can produce thousands of impressions per minute. But offset printing has high setup costs. Creating printing plates and setting up the inks and the presses is expensive (paper is expensive no matter what way you print). Once everything is set up, the per-unit price goes down the more copies you order. A thousand books might cost three dollars apiece, but if you go for two thousand books, you can have them for a dollar fifty each. Around the turn of the (twenty-first) century, publishers who wanted to print fewer than five hundred copies of a book had a hard time finding a printer willing to take their business. With the development of laser, inkjet, and digital printing technologies, options for professional-quality short-run printing finally emerged, called short-run digital printing (SRDP). Print on demand (POD), in which a book isn't produced until someone has ordered it, has taken us to the shortest possible run: one book at a time.

Early on, the difference in quality between offset and digital printing processes was significant enough for publishers to stay away. Academic presses were some of the first adopters, digital being a good fit for books that have a small, specialized audience and a high price point. Eventually trade publishers saw the obvious benefits and began to use digital production to print advanced reader copies (ARCs) for review and to fill in between offset print runs. More significantly, digital printing allows publishers to maintain an eternal backlist and resurrect books that may have long been out of print. Books that sell only a handful of copies a year, and may not have been considered worth the cost of a print run or warehousing, can now be held in wait as digital files, ready to be printed, bound, and shipped when ordered.[11]

For small publishers, digital printing—and the ability to do very short runs or even single print-on-demand copies—opens up options and opportunities. Instead of laying out a big sum for printing, they can do a smaller print run or even no print run, as they wait and see how books sell. And the explosion of author-directed self-publishing is possible only because POD technology requires no upfront investment, nor the need to store or distribute physical books.

Digital printing is still in its adolescence. Many people are satisfied with the look of digital printing for one-color, text-driven books, and some argue it has reached parity with offset printing even for illustrated and other books where print quality is important. As in any situation, different printers will produce different quality products. Just because digital *can* look as good as offset doesn't mean that it always does. Also, trim sizes, paper choices, binding, and finishing effects are all more limited in digital than in offset. Different brands and models of printers have different strengths and weaknesses, and it may be hard for publishers or authors to know what they're signing up for. And books printed on demand can go out into the world with very few eyes on them. Errors happen in all printing scenarios, but books that are printed days or months apart, as they are in POD, will have different issues with different operators at different times. One copy looks great, and the next is bound in upside down and backward.

I recently ordered a book online (direct from the publisher, of course), and when it arrived the paper was tissue-thin and bright white, and the printing looked like it had been Xeroxed by my high school biology teacher in 1985. The book, which I had been eager to read, got plonked on the stack, where it remains. It's just not inviting. A reader is going to spend hours and hours with your book (you hope). Quality production and materials make a difference not only in the bookstore, but at home on the sofa.

Chapter 2

Type

You can't understand the basics of book design without knowing a little about type, so here goes: Letters have a life apart from type. Your signature, scratches on the bathroom wall, and your shopping list are made of letters, but not of type (unless your shopping list is on your phone, in which case it is).

Type is a specific form of letter making: mechanized, idealized, and reproducible. It's all around us: on your driver's license, paychecks, the menu over the registers at Taco Bell. It appears on billboards, parking tickets, street signs, newspapers, money, the letter from the utility company, the barely visible ingredients on the back of the shampoo bottle, advertising flyers, political placards, "no smoking" signs, the hours for the laundromat, the buttons on the dishwasher, the front of my T-shirt ("Nevertheless, she persisted"). It's in emails, tweets, websites, movie titles, candy bar wrappers, bumper stickers. It's what you're looking at right now.

Type is made using fonts. Most writers and editors are familiar with fonts—they inhabit a drop-down menu in the word processing programs we all spend so much of our lives using. You may have even developed some opinions—know the names of some fonts, perhaps have a favorite to write in, or know which ones you are supposed to look down your nose at. So you're aware that fonts have personalities or flavors, that they're expressive, aesthetic things. (The most famous quote in typography is from the font designer Eric Gill: "Letters are things, not pictures of things." Chew on that for a while.[1]) Which fonts are used, and how, is elemental to the spirit of what's being said. A receipt from the grocery store, set in a fancy script centered like a wedding invitation, would be unhelpful indeed. No different with book design. For each book, and each part of each book, type should be well chosen, well matched, and well used.

Brief History

Before the invention of type, books were written out longhand by professional scribes, which was a very slow process. Only a select few, mostly rich, people ever got to read, much less own, one of these treasures. (Of course, very few people knew how to read.) But still the demand for books was larger than the scribes could supply. Johannes Gutenberg didn't actually invent the printing press, but he did bring together technologies in a time and place—Mainz, Germany, circa 1450—that was primed for them.[2]

The press Gutenberg used was a screw press, like those common at the time for pressing grapes for wine or olives for oil.[3] He also created a printer's ink, adapted from paint, that was stiff and would adhere to metal.[4] And the type! Gutenberg had worked as a goldsmith, and cutting type is a kind of metal work—carving intricate shapes into the tiny face of a little metal bar. The initial engraved object is called the punch and it is hammered into another piece of metal, called the matrix, producing a negative of the letter. That negative is placed at the bottom of a mold (some say that the design of the mold was Gutenberg's most important contribution to the development of printing) through which liquid metal is poured with a ladle. The metal sets and can be popped out in a matter of seconds—there's that beautiful letter B—to make copy after copy of the character. Those pieces of finished type are arranged, printed, and then put away to be reused for the next job.

Once the punches are made, a near-endless amount of type can be cast. Once the type is cast, a near-endless number of words—and books and other things—can be printed. And once that happens, ideas can be broadcast far and wide and into the future, in near-infinite reverberations. One person's thoughts, stories, poetry, jokes, declarations, philosophies, rules, contracts, recipes, and revolutionary provocations could reach a stranger halfway around the world, or one thousand strangers, or a hundred thousand. Printing with type was a seismic shift in the history of humanity and is critical to the shape of the world in which we all now live.

Metal Type

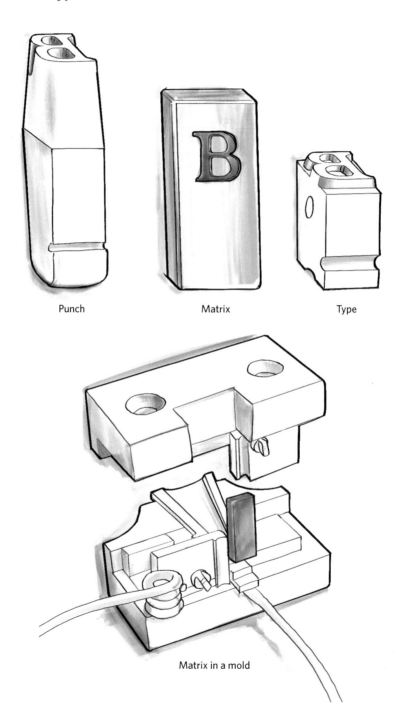

Punch   Matrix   Type

Matrix in a mold

As more books became available, more people (mostly men) learned to read. Printers sprouted up all around Germany and then Italy and then elsewhere in Europe. (In the first fifty years after Gutenberg some twelve million books were printed in Europe.[5]) Every press needed an alphabetic set of type to print with, and, voilà: fonts! Printers bought or created (or hired someone to create) their type, and, naturally, some were more and some less skilled. The first printed books were trying to approximate handwritten ones, which were of higher status, and their type mimicked the stylized handwriting of professional scribes.[6] Gutenberg's Bible—the first European book printed with type—was set in a style that is called blackletter. It's heavy, compressed, and pointy. There were a bunch of variations on this style of type, many very beautiful. But not very easy to read.

Within twenty years another style arose, which we call roman (lowercase *r*). The capitals of roman letters were based on letters inscribed in ancient Roman monuments; the lowercase on another style of handwriting (Carolingian minuscules, if you must know). The forms of these letters were finer, rounder, more open, more distinct from each other than the blackletter forms and became the blueprint for type set in the Latin alphabet for the next five hundred years (and counting). Probably every book you've ever read—including this one—was set in roman type.

Like all art forms, type has evolved in response to changing audiences, technologies, opportunities, and culture. It is also the product of the minds and hands of individual humans.[7] The changes may seem subtle because type design is necessarily conservative and type is just so tiny. The most avant-garde designer can get only so out there and still have a shape *be* a certain letter, or be recognized as such, which is the same thing.

lte orucltct œc quuqer gar lttt·
nd to iacob horet das man in rgípt
kaufft·Do spzach rr zu seiné suñ· I
pta und kaufft uns auch kozn das wir í
sterben· Do furn ir zehé in egipto und br
min to heim·Dnd to sie zu ioseph komé

The earliest European type looked like this: blackletter.

HERBE CHE NASC/
NO APPVNTATE
Eguitano herbe lequali per
& maxime in Egypto abbõ

Within twenty years, roman type developed, and it looked basically the same for the next four hundred years.

Every age and generation
must be as free to act for
itself in all cases as the age

By the late eighteenth century, roman type had gotten very stylized. This high-contrast look was the fashion. Note the hairlines on the horizontal strokes.

Worms have played a more
important part in the history o
the world than most persons

In the nineteenth century, sans serifs arrived.

LOVE YOUR
MOTHER

In the twentieth century, "geometric" sans derived from geometric shapes rather than handwriting. Notice how the o is an almost perfect circle.

The quick brown fox
jumps over the lazy dog

By the mid-1990s, type was being designed not in metal but on computers. Comic Sans is one of thousands of examples that demonstrate the freedom of designing type digitally.

Letter Anatomy

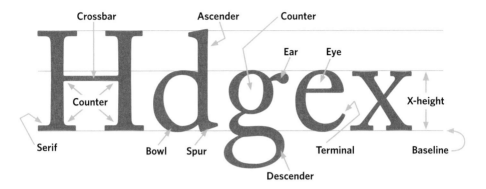

Looking at Letters

The way that letters are formed impacts their legibility and their character, as you well know from the difference between your teacher's and your little brother's handwriting. Same goes for type. Letters look different in different typefaces. The stems of an uppercase *M* might be splayed or straight up and down. A lowercase *g* can be double-bowled or open. A lowercase *a* is sometimes two-storied, sometimes single-storied. The leg of the uppercase *R* can do all manner of kicks off the bowl. And the tails of a capital *Q* are as variable (and charming) as the tails of different breeds of dogs.

Naming things helps us see them, and identifying the parts of the letter will help you notice their differences. This is particularly helpful when comparing or talking about fonts with a designer (or showing off at a dinner party). The lines and curves of letters are referred to as their strokes, whether written with a pen or printed in type. The space within a letter, whether closed like an uppercase *D* or open like an uppercase *H*, is called its counter. Because details can be hard to see at text size, it's rewarding to blow up a few letters or words and really check out their look. Even more illuminating is setting the same letters next to each other in different fonts. Letters that had seemed nearly identical reveal themselves to be wonderfully diverse.[8]

Font Categories

When you are writing in Microsoft Word or Google Docs or Scrivener, you have a set of fonts provided to you for free as part of the software package. Designers range much wider—seeking out specific typefaces for specific jobs or browsing for new fonts looking for ideas and inspiration. Typeface design is a booming area and there are a lot of fonts out there. Many websites sell fonts, while others, including Google, offer them for free. The font marketplace forces you to understand something about how fonts are made and packaged—for instance, you can buy just the bold weight of a typeface, just the italic, just the bold italic. And the sticker price (of some fonts) might make you realize the amount of work, and artistry, that goes into their creation. Browse any font-selling website and you'll see they're generally organized in broad categories based on how they look and how they're used. Here are the basics.

Serif

Gargoyle

Sans Serif

Gargoyle

Italic

Gargoyle

Blackletter

Gargoyle

Script

Gargoyle

Casual Script

Serif

Serif fonts are the most common type of type, used for setting long passages of text in books, magazines, manuals, newspapers, reports, letters, and most everything else. College essays, dissertations, and book manuscripts are often required to be set in a serifed type (often 12-point Times New Roman), and typeset books usually have the main text in a serif font. Serif type can also be used for display, as on book covers. You might associate serifed type with history or literature, but probably it just seems "normal"—what you expect print to look like.

What the heck is a serif? Serifs are the little ticks or wedges or feet that appear at the ends of the main strokes, including on the letters you are reading now. Serifs add structure and liveliness to letters, help distinguish them from each other, and reinforce the horizontal movement of text. Although they're widely believed to make reading more efficient, there is some dispute over whether they actually do so.[9]

As small as they are, and as similar as they may appear to the untrained eye, serifs have a lot of variety and character. They can be hairline thin, moderate, or dramatically thick. They can be wedge shaped, cupped, flat slabs, or calligraphic zings. They can sit horizontally or slope up toward the next letter. Their particularities give them personality. See some examples on the following page.

Sans Serif

Sans means "without," so sans serif fonts are literally letters without serifs. At the end of their strokes they just, uh, end. Sans serif typefaces were developed and used widely for advertising in the nineteenth century, when they were called grotesques in Europe and gothics in the US. If you see a font with *Gothic* hitched to its name (Trade Gothic, News Gothic, and Franklin Gothic are all popular fonts), it is stylistically based on these older sans serifs. Highway Gothic, designed in the 1940s for the United States Federal Highway Administration, is still used on every highway sign across America. There are other kinds of sans serifs, including geometric (Futura is the archetype) and humanistic (Gill Sans is a popular example). I presume you have heard of Helvetica, probably the most widely used font ever.[10]

The Wide World of Serifs

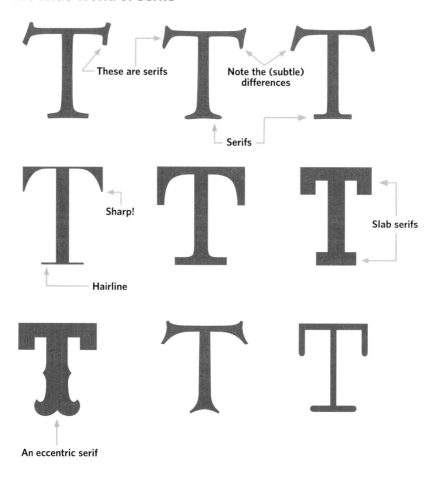

These are serifs

Note the (subtle) differences

Serifs

Sharp!

Hairline

Slab serifs

An eccentric serif

Sans serifs are stripped down, unfussy, and, as a result, impactful. They can embody the cool aesthetic of modernism or the more neutral sensibility of corporate branding and communication. They're versatile and can look great extra bold or hairline thin, condensed, compressed, or extended. Sans serifs are commonly used for display purposes (see page 44) and are all over the place on book covers.

Although sans serifs may be easy to read even at small sizes, they tend not to be used for long passages of type in print. But they still serve an important function inside books. Contrast is an essential element of typography (more on that to come), and sans serifs are an excellent foil to the serif type used for most text in most books. They're effective for emphasis, distinction of elements, and flashes of power. It is rare that I design a book without at least one serif and one sans serif font.

Italic

Most people think of italic as something you *do* to type, a toggle on the menu bar—bold/italic/underline. Oh, but no. Italic type is a thing unto itself. (So is bold for that matter. Conflating underline, something you do to type, with bold and italic, which are *kinds* of type, is one of the most egregious typographic crimes committed by word processing software.) Around 1500, the inventive publisher Aldus Manutius had the idea to create books that were not so big they required a table to hold them up. Small, light, and therefore portable, these books could be tucked into your doublet and carried about town. To make the best use of space, he wanted type that would pack as many words as possible on the page. The result was an italic.

Italic type is based on cursive handwriting and is structurally distinct from its upright cousin. It's not just roman type set on a slope. Italic type is traditionally narrow, the letters snuggly fit, making it compact and efficient. Entire books were set in italic during the Renaissance, and even when roman and italic were, eventually, used within the same book, they were kept apart—certain text set in roman only and other in italic only. When typographers started mixing the two, and found the pairing lively and functional, italic morphed into the role it serves in contemporary books and elsewhere—as companion (and, let's face it, underling) to roman type, used for emphasis or differentiation of words or passages.

No serious font family would appear without an italic variation, as italic type is used all over the place in book design. How italics and romans are matched—the degree of congruence or contrast between the two—affects the look of a book page, particularly if italics are in heavy rotation. Italic type sits prettily within lines of text, emphasizing words and phrases or calling out titles or non-English words. It can also be used for quoted material and epigraphs, headings, and running heads (see chapter 4), as well as other areas where designers want to create a contrast to the upright, or roman, text. That said, I tend to avoid using italic for long passages of text. Its tight, calligraphic nature can make it hard reading over the long haul (although some italics are more legible than others). When contrast is needed for more than a phrase or two—say for a chapter intended to show a different voice or narrator—I will usually pick a sans serif over italic (other designers, of course, may make other choices).

Scripts and Handwriting Faces

Italics are based on handwriting, but scripts are facsimiles of it. Historically, scripts tend to be highly formal and quite decorative— think wedding invitations—imitating the most elegant handwriting of their time. They can be idiosyncratic and challenging to read and so have limited use in book design and elsewhere. It wasn't until the late twentieth century that more casual handwriting scripts proliferated, ushered in, in part, by the success of the snobbishly despised Comic Sans. These typefaces mimic everyday handwriting, sign painting, graffiti, and chalkboard menus. The popularity of actual hand lettering on book covers (and packaging and advertising, and so forth) and the availability of font creation software has led to an avalanche of handwriting-style typefaces—fonts that are meant to appear as if they're written but are actually type. (I discuss the difference between type and lettering in the next chapter.) Many of them are lovely, but they're distincly not handwriting. Even the most smartly engineered typeface cannot fully embody the natural idiosyncrasy of the hand.

Casual scripts are currently popular in book design, especially on covers (romance novels are lousy with casual scripts) and also for certain kinds of interiors where a friendly or homespun vibe is desired. When working with scripts and handwriting-style fonts, I'm always attuned to legibility, suitability, and tone. Even when designing books for children, cutesy isn't a winning approach and can undermine when communicating words meant to be taken seriously, as almost all words in all books are.

Typeface versus Font

The words *typeface* and *font* are often used interchangeably but are not exactly the same. Caslon is a typeface, for example, and 12-point Caslon bold is a font. A font is like the set of pieces in a specific chess set, like the one that was on the shelf in your fifth-grade classroom. A typeface is like Milton Bradley's chess sets as opposed to Staunton's chess sets—they contain the same array of recognizable pieces (their alphabets) but each has its own particular look.

In the days of metal type, this distinction mattered. An author might go to a print shop and say, "I'd like my book set in Caslon," and the printer might say, "Splendid, I am an admirer of that typeface. I've got two fonts: 10 point and 12 point." Then the author might say, "Sir! I always insist on 11-point Caslon!" And the printer would say, "Well, I guess you're out of luck. I don't have that font."

In the digital age, the fonts we use are computer files. I don't have stacked cases of metal type in my office, but thousands of files on my computer. If I've got the file for Caslon, I've got the typeface *and* I've got the font. What was a useful difference in terminology has become, in most situations, irrelevant. In my world, the terms *font* and *typeface* (or just *type*) are used interchangeably all the time without confusion. Feel free to do the same.

Blackletter

The earliest type in Europe, Gutenberg's type, is what we now call blackletter. This style was used widely throughout Europe in the early days of printing and held on in Germany into the twentieth century, eventually outlawed by the Nazis. Its look is related to the Gothic style in art and architecture (imagine Notre Dame as a capital *M*). Blackletter is seen today mostly on the mastheads of newspapers and the logos of heavy metal bands, but type designers continue to design new fonts in this style. While some type designers have worked to make highly legible blackletter faces, and they occasionally appear on book covers, there's not much occasion for use of blackletter as body copy in books. Do you want to read the latest Franzen in even a highly legible blackletter?

Text Type versus Display Type

The categories I've discussed so far are basic ways of grouping fonts, but there's an even simpler formulation: text type versus display type. It's probably obvious that type used for display on book covers is more varied in style than that used inside a book. There are many different text types and they all have their particularities and personalities, but, for most people, they look pretty much the same. Their job is to deliver the news, not be the news, and to do this they should look how we expect, do what we need, and fade into the background. (The primary text in a book can also be called body type or sometimes running text, both terms I use throughout this book.) Text types are mostly serifed, although in the twentieth century some sans serif faces were designed for use in long passages of text, and you will run into these occasionally. The designer Michael Bierut tells a story about another designer, Tibor Kalman, who was "fascinated with boring typefaces. 'No, this one is too clever, this one is too interesting,' he kept saying when I showed him the fonts I was proposing for his monograph. Anything but a boring typeface, he felt, got in the way of the ideas."[11]

Type for display purposes—not just on covers but also for chapter titles and other headings—can be more diverse than text type, less self-effacing, weirder. It's usually set larger than text type and that alone gives it some formal leeway. Display types can be serif or sans, blackletter or script. Some nifty font families include both display and "book" variations and can work well in both contexts—their details and character emerging as they're set at larger sizes. In the majority of cases, display fonts will be as respectable and readable as any other. But they can also push the limits and forgo absolute devotion to clarity in pursuit of other goals like experimentation, expressiveness, or ornamentation. One of the pleasures of selecting type for book covers is that I can be open to decorative and quirky fonts that would never work for extended reading inside the book. Book covers want, in part, to stand out. Unusual or interesting title type is one way to accomplish this.

The Character Set

What comes in the box with your shiny new font? Books have long and complex texts and the character set of a font is an important factor in determining its suitability for any given project. What is immediately visible on a keyboard is but a modicum of the possible characters available. What follows are the general categories of characters, or glyphs, that may or may not be included with any given font.

The Alphabet

When most people think of a font, they think of letters. Most fonts intended for use in books include a triple alphabet—full sets of lowercase and uppercase letters and a set of small caps (there is also such a thing as medium caps, but they're rare). Type nerds like to point out that the terms *lowercase* and *uppercase* come from the physical trays—cases—that hold individual pieces of metal type in a print shop. The capitals (if you are stuffy, you can call them majuscules) are housed in the upper case and the small letters (minuscules) in the lower one. Uppercase and lowercase letters are distinguished by size and by function ("the upper case has seniority but the lower case has the power"[12]). Uppercase letters are the same height, lining up in a neat row when set next to one another. Lowercase letters are all arms and legs, not as tidy but easier to pick out due to their more distinctive shapes. Small caps retain the uniform height and form of uppercase letters but are the size of lowercase letters. Small caps are a nice way to render words in all caps that are set within running text—for instance "The sign said REWARD!" They make their point without screaming in your ear.

The English alphabet contains twenty-six letters, but many other languages that use the Latin alphabet have additional characters and use diacritics (marks that appear above, below, or within a letter). Many fonts will include a minimal number of these (most commonly the tilde, umlaut, and grave and acute accents), and some contain a smorgasbord. When I'm designing books that use a lot of non-English words, the extent of the character set will be a deciding factor in my choice of typeface.

Ligatures

A ligature is the combination of two or three letters into a single unit, most commonly *ff*, *fi*, *fl*, *ffi*, and *ffl*. You'll notice that all these begin with the lowercase *f*. The top of that letter invades the space of the letter following it and, if that letter sticks up—hello *i* and *l*—it can crash into it in unseemly ways. Most fonts include at least these five standard ligatures, and professional typesetting software can be set to automatically replace these letter combinations with the appropriate ligature. There are many other ligatures as well—some necessary for non-English alphabets (e.g., the *œ* combination in French) and some ornamental (like the combined *Th* in some fonts). While the lowercase *f* series is standard usage, ornamental ligatures are a judgment call, sometimes too fancy (distracting) for use in body text. When setting display type for titles, though, ornamental ligatures can add surprise or elegance, and I might choose a font based on a particularly appealing ligature for a letter combination that appears in a title.

ff fi fl ffi ffl

Standard English ligatures

Th Æ æ ch ck œ sp st tt

Some other possible ligatures

Numerals

Groomed to type on a computer keyboard or, before that, a typewriter, most folks are aware of only one set of numerals. Whether or not this was a capitalist plot can be debated, but like letters, numerals—both arabic and roman—have *two* cases. Uppercase numerals are usually called lining (as in aligning) or titling numerals and are of uniform height, the same as the uppercase set of letters. Lowercase numerals are referred to as oldstyle or text numerals and correspond to the size and variability of lowercase letters. The most useful fonts come with both. General design practice is to use uppercase numerals with uppercase type and lowercase most other times. In tables or equations where numbers should line up or in lists of measurements—say an ingredient list or sewing pattern—I will often choose lining numerals for their uniformity and prominence.

0123456789   0123456789

Oldstyle numerals   Lining numerals

Punctuation

Writers and editors are highly aware of the subtleties and importance of punctuation. Who hasn't agonized over the implications wrought by the use of a semicolon versus an em dash? Designers take these marks seriously as well. Some display typefaces include a very limited set of punctuation, little more than a comma and a period. Fonts meant for use inside books need to come fully loaded.

Punctuation marks look different in different fonts, and I try to avoid a page littered with ugly commas. Quotation marks (and the commas they're identical to) range from plump to scrawny; some are periods with tails, others more like little ticks or slashes. Question marks—so expressive both literally and visually—can be sinuous like a backward *S* or shaped more like a pirate's hook. Parentheses can bulge in the middle or retain an even stroke from top to bottom. A period might be oval rather than circular, or even, in some fonts, diamond-shaped or square. Hyphens and dashes must be carefully sized in relation to each other. A stubby em dash might be confusing and will prompt concerned queries from the proofreader. Fractions are often problematic and can be too small or the numbers unevenly positioned with respect to the slash (important in books with lots of ¼ cups of flour). The heroic ampersand—perhaps typography's most delightful mark—can take on all sorts of wild configurations.

These are all commas.

Punctuation marks should not be afterthoughts. Their presence facilitates our understanding, editorially and visually. When they're out of sync with the words and sentences around them, they become dysfunctional.

Other Characters

There are a host of characters that aren't punctuation, numbers, or letters. Some of them reside on the keyboard; many are hidden behind a secret door (take a look at the advanced symbol panel in Word). The percent sign, the dollar sign, the degree symbol, the "at" symbol, the copyright symbol, and the now-ubiquitous hash tag (virtually an honorary alphabetic character) are all characters that can and do appear in books. Like all aspects of a typeface, these marks can be more or less carefully designed and made to fit with the set as a whole.

There is also a category of symbols that are intended for use alongside type, often referred to as ornaments or dingbats. These might be arrows, stars, pointing hands, check marks, leaves, geometric shapes, card suits, decorative lines, or pictograms of a phone, a pencil, or a scissors. They are used to fill space, to delineate sections, or simply to decorate. Many fonts contain a handful of these symbols. There are also fonts that are made up solely of symbols—the classic is the 1970s font Zapf Dingbats—which can be used in partnership with any other font.

Some common dingbats

The Family

Roman and italic type were developed independent of each other. Books were printed for four hundred years before bold appeared and it was another hundred years before bold italic was widely used.[13] It wasn't until 1957, and the design of Adrian Frutiger's typeface Univers, that the concept of a font family—a set of coordinated fonts that share structural and stylistic qualities—became a thing.[14] Nowadays, it's not only common but expected.

Font Families

Garamond* Regular	Trade Gothic Light
Garamond Italic	Trade Gothic Regular
GARAMOND SMALL CAPS	*Trade Gothic Oblique*
Garamond Semibold	**Trade Gothic Bold**
Garamond Semibold Italic	***Trade Gothic Bold Oblique***
Garamond Bold	Trade Gothic Condensed
Garamond Bold Italic	*Trade Gothic Condensed Oblique*
	Trade Gothic Bold Condensed
	Trade Gothic Bold Condensed Ol
	Trade Gothic Extende
	Trade Gothic Bold Ex

*There are a lot of versions of Garamond out there. What you see here is Garamond Premier designed by Robert Slimbach.

What's included in a font's family differs from typeface to type-face. A bold and italic face are generally required for any typeface meant to be used inside a book. Some include condensed, com-pressed, and extended styles, while others are focused on a light-to-extra-bold continuum. Some megafamilies will include both serif and sans serif variations, or even an accompanying script. Above are some of the more common variations you find in a robust font family. (Note the term *oblique* used with Trade Gothic in the illustration above. The "italic" of sans serif fonts is often a sloped version of the roman, rather than a true italic, and this is indicated by the word *oblique*.)

Choosing Type

I'll choose a typeface because I use it all the time, or I'll choose one because I've never used it before. Sometimes I'll choose a typeface because it's fashionable and other times because it's so basic that it never goes into or out of vogue. I'll see a new font used beautifully in another book, or elsewhere, and then hunt it down so I can use it too. I'll see a classic or tired font used in a new or surprising way and be inspired to use it that way as well. There are some fonts I never choose.

Picking fonts is something designers sweat over, and enjoy. There are so many fonts to comb through, and we know—or at least believe—that the fonts we pick matter, that different choices will create different experiences for the reader. The typography guru Robert Bringhurst said it more beautifully than I can: "Letterforms have tone, timbre, character, just as words and sentences do. The moment a text and a typeface are chosen, two streams of thought, two rhythmical systems, two sets of habits, or if you like, two personalities, intersect."[15] So how to decide? Here are some of the things I think about.

Functionality

I'll get the practical stuff out of the way first. For type inside the book, a designer needs to consider: What kind of text is there? Are there many non-English words? Numbers, math, measurements, tables? Captions? Twenty layers of hierarchy? How old are the readers (and how strong is their eyesight)? Do I need to cram a lot of words into a limited space? Is the detective agency called Miller & Son, and I get to use an ampersand? Is the main character named Quimby and uppercase Q's will be scattered everywhere? (In some fonts the tail of the Q is really prominent and will make an impression on a page. Is that welcome or not?) These most pragmatic of decisions make up the first round of winnowing. I once designed a book that contained song lyrics in more than twenty-five languages, and I spent a long time hunting for a font that had every character and diacritic I needed. When working on books with lots of numbers, I look carefully at both sets of numerical figures and the way fractions look. The numeral 1, in particular, can look, in some fonts, too similar to an uppercase *I* or a lowercase *l*, and if this is going to cause ambiguity or confusion, that typeface will be disqualified.

Tone

They might all look the same to you, but to designers different fonts have distinctly different feels. I'm always trying to match the sense I have of a typeface with the sense I have of a text. A font can seem classic or old-fashioned, elegant or friendly, energetic or even harsh. The shapes of the letters, the shapes of the serifs, the lack of serifs, the degree of stress or slope, the level of contrast all contribute to a sensibility that, consciously or not, adds texture and tone to a title, passage, or entire body of text. Most designers will set a block of text in one typeface, then another, then another, looking for that "click," the feeling that the type is the right vessel for the words. (Choosing a type is just step one, then there's choosing the size and the spacing and *treatment* of the type.) As in all creative pursuits, there's more than one answer, more than one avenue. A text might work beautifully in a traditional typeface (and designed in a classic setting) and also in something cooler or more contemporary. Which way you go depends on what you are trying to *do*. Simon & Garfunkel do one thing with "Bridge over Troubled Water" and Aretha Franklin does another.

Origins

When a type was designed, where, by whom, and in what cultural context are all possible considerations when picking fonts for a project. Books that refer explicitly to historic eras, events, or people might be paired with a geographically or period-appropriate typeface (a book on Benjamin Franklin should certainly be paired with his favorite typeface, Baskerville). In a book highlighting the achievements of women, say, it could be nice to choose a font designed by one. The same is true for other markers of identity. Most fonts boast about their history or influences on font-selling websites. There are also plenty of books and websites that discuss historical fonts and review new ones. Many designers think about the origins of a typeface before they sic it on a text. I (usually) won't buy a font without knowing who made it and when.

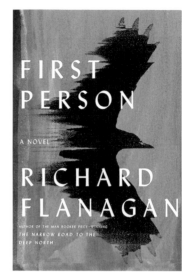

The font Lydian, then and now.

Fashion

Like all cultural products, typefaces go in and out of fashion. Particularly for display type, certain fonts have their moments and sometimes look dated afterward. The 1950s and '60s were crazy for cool sans serifs like Futura and Helvetica (think *Mad Men*). The 1970s were all wide-collared shirts and eccentric serifed fonts. The digital revolution begat a slew of grungy, degraded type. Twenty-first-century typefaces (ironically) celebrate the handmade and "authentic" with a thousand faux-handwriting fonts.

When styles that arose in one period are used in an entirely different context, the new meaning can stick. Who would have predicted that the ridiculed mom jeans of the 1980s would become a hip style for teens in the 2010s? Fonts created with one logic in the early-twentieth-century Bauhaus art movement were reimagined as spacey and futuristic for sci-fi movies in the 1960s and '70s.[16] The calligraphic font Lydian, designed in 1938, was popular on the covers of pulp novels and the *Nancy Drew* series in the 1950s. Fifty years on, it has been revitalized as type for literary and serious book covers and is all over the New Releases table at Barnes & Noble.[17] Contemporary viewers probably think of this font as very "now"—it is! And it isn't! Unlike 78-rpm records, old fonts don't get worn out or sold at yard sales. If they've been digitized, they're always available to us and, thus, always available for reassessment.

Familiarity

Most designers sprinkle in the occasional new typeface with a pantry of staples. My go-to fonts aren't necessarily better than other ones I could choose, but I know them well (have sought them out and paid for them), and that counts for a lot. For text type, particularly, it's a lot of work to learn the ins and outs of a new typeface. It's like a new car that you don't really know until you've driven it a thousand miles. I could be halfway through typesetting a book when I realize I hate its fractions. There are designers who work with the same small group of typefaces for decades. The designer of the New York City subway map, Massimo Vignelli, was famous for claiming that six typefaces—Bodoni, Garamond, Century Expanded, Futura, Times New Roman, and Helvetica—were sufficient for every and any possible use over a lifetime of work (and this wasn't limited to book design).[18] That's an extreme example, but a long-term relationship is one of the best reasons I can think of to work with a particular typeface.

Screen Fonts

Books don't come only on paper anymore. Ebooks use typography as extensively as printed books do, and type designers have developed fonts that are optimized for viewing on screens. In the mid-1990s, when it became clear what the internet was going to mean for all of us, the designer Matthew Carter developed the first fonts specifically for use on screens—Georgia, a serif, and Verdana, a sans serif. At the time, fonts that were created to be printed with ink at high resolution were being used at quite low resolution on screens, hence the pixelated or bitmapped look of early computing. Among other technical accomplishments, Carter placed an emphasis on the white space within and between letters to ensure that forms were legible and differentiated from each other even at low resolution. (These typefaces are still widely popular for use on screen and in print, and you may be familiar with them.) The technology for how fonts are drawn and displayed has improved and many fonts followed, including, eventually, Amazon's proprietary ebook fonts Bookerly and Ember and Google's (open-source) Literata. Despite the implications of user-defined font choice for ebooks (more about that in chapter 6), if designers are picking type for reading on screen, they smartly lean toward type choices that are designed for that environment.

Using Fonts Together

It's certainly possible—and in type scholarship often considered admirable—to set an entire book in a single typeface. More commonly, I want two or three fonts for all the different situations inside a book. Usually, I will choose a serifed text type for the body text and a sans serif as a contrast for chapter titles and headings. Sometimes the diversity of text will make the addition of a third font appropriate—for sidebars or other distinctive passages, as display type in part or chapter openers, or for small areas of emphasis or little areas of flair. This is (usually) enough. Font choice isn't the only way to differentiate kinds of text, and designers push type to show its many faces by using it bold or in all caps or larger or, when possible, in color. Keeping a font palette limited makes a big project feel unified and intentional. (For a discussion of choosing type for covers, see page 82.)

Fonts set together in a book should make a handsome couple (or ménage à trois): they need to look good sitting next to each other at the bar. That relationship might be one of analogy or one of contrast. Usually there are some elements of both. Trying out different fonts on the page together reveals a lot about the flavor of each. I hadn't realized how spikey or wide or calligraphic this one was until I set it next to that one. Mixing and matching is part experience and part experimentation. Covers are usually designed first, and if there's a distinctive font used on a cover, I might bring it inside for my chapter titles. (Even if it's not particularly distinctive, I will often use it inside to create cohesion between outside and inside of the book.) This will set a tone around which I can choose my other fonts.

If a book mixes languages and a second font is required for non-Latin characters—let's say in Japanese—matching the style and spirit (and scale) of Latin and non-Latin fonts is as important as any other pairing. If the book is primarily in English, non-English words shouldn't shout out their difference but should flow naturally within the text.

Type Size

Many people know that there is the number 12 next to "Arial" along the menu bar in Word. This can be decreased to 10 or increased to 14 and the font on your screen gets smaller or larger accordingly. This is a change to the font's point size, the traditional unit of measurement for type. (Type for use on screens, like for ebooks, is usually measured relatively, in percentages or *ems*.) Writers change their font's size, and designers do this as well.

There are 72 points to an inch—12-point text will be about ⅙ inch from the top of the lowercase *h* to the bottom of the lowercase *p*. In the days of metal type, point size was really important. Printers ordered their fonts by point size: "I'd like a set of 12-point Garamond, please." In the digital age, any font can be displayed at any size, and designers are free to decide whether they want to set their text at 11.25 or 11.5 or 11.75 (we really do work in increments of tenths of a point). With freedom comes responsibility. Fonts that are designed to work at text sizes can lose their shape when presented large. Fonts designed for display use are often hard to read small and not suitable for body text. Designers take care to understand how a font is meant to function and use it appropriately.

The fact is that the number doesn't matter much. You know that the medium sweatpants from Old Navy don't fit the same as the mediums from the Gap, and fonts act similarly. How open the forms are, how wide, how stubby or long the ascenders and descenders and the size of the x-height (the height of the lowercase letters excluding their extenders, or the size of the lowercase *x*) affects the *perceived* size of a font. Fonts with a taller x-height are usually considered more readable. They also will appear larger at the same point size. Times New Roman set at 12 points does not look the same as Arial set at 12 points and in fact doesn't take up the same amount of space. And type size is only one of several factors that determine how well type reads and how hierarchy is established (I'll explore the other aspects in chapter 4). Point size is useful notation, but not that meaningful. Designers use their eyes, not the drop-down menu, to make judgments around size and all other questions of style.

Times New Roman (in black) and Arial (in red) at the same point size.

Styling Type

Which typeface at what size are only the most basic questions for a designer. Once I've picked a type I can adjust all sorts of things about it: its case; its weight; whether some words are set in italics, or all the words; how much space appears between the letters; or how the text breaks into shorter lines. A font may have one personality at extra bold and a totally different one in a light weight. All caps always feels different from title case. The treatment of type, and the contrasting treatment of type, gives it a style but also imparts meaning. Bolder, bigger words stick out more and are understood to be more important. A visual shift is itself "content." (Shifts should always be strong enough to be clearly intentional. I never want the reader to wonder, "Is that smaller or is it just me?") Type *styling* and type *treatment* (terms I use interchangeably) come up a lot in this book. They're a fundamental part of design expression.

greatest of all time

Greatest *of* All Time

GREATEST OF ALL TIME

Greatest of ALL time

greatest
OF ALL TIME

Greatest of
all time

**GREATEST
OF
ALL
TIME**

GREATEST
OF
ALL TIME

**GREATEST
OF ALL TIME**

The examples above all use the same two typefaces—a serif and a sans serif.
The choices around boldness, color, size, case, and where lines break
affect the mood and how the words are understood.

Chapter 3
The Cover

Your editor will tell you that your book's cover is its best marketing tool, and it surely plays that role. Propped on tables or in the window of a bookstore, books cry out, "Pick me! Pick me!" They're dying to catch your eye and tell you about themselves. Their titles, type, art (or lack thereof), and colors are marriages of beauty and information. Popping up in our social media feeds, news sites, and everywhere online, book covers look so good and promise so much. Adam Gopnik writes, "Book covers may be inessential to the primary task of reading books, and yet they are invaluable to the secondary task, making books appealing and seductive by their shimmer."[1]

But book covers are more than just a lure. They hang around—on our coffee tables, on our bookshelves, and in our minds. When searching for any book in my chaotic bookcase, I have a perfect idea of what color it is and the way the title appears on the spine. The cover for V. C. Andrews's *Flowers in the Attic*—with its creepy illustration and peekaboo die cut—will transport me right back to Michigan, 1980. Spotting someone on the bus holding a familiar cover is like recognizing a face in a crowd. A cover is more than an advertisement; it is a book's visual identity.

This chapter explains how (most) book covers get made—the external forces that shape them and the elements of craft that bring them into being. Cover design isn't simply a visual interpretation of a text—as if that's not hard enough—but must respond to a chorus of voices telling it how to be. The marketing manager wants to add a blurb, the editor decides a longer subtitle is necessary, the author insists that their sister's watercolor is the perfect image, and the publisher wants it to resemble the bestselling books in the category. Some designs click in the first or second round of review. Others can take a dozen iterations before a final version is approved. As the designer Rodrigo Corral put it: "Can't be a good cover, has to be the right cover."[2]

What's on a Cover

While I spend a lot of time figuring out what *might* appear on a cover—how to visualize ideas that took an author 100,000 words to explain—I must also figure out what to do with what *must* appear there. Most book covers feature a standard set of elements that are decided upon, after much thought and discussion, by the author, editor, and marketing team. Title, subtitle, the name of the author, and every other piece of text affect both the general direction of a cover and the minutiae of its execution. A one-word title requires a different cover approach than a six-word title. A reading line or none, a long subtitle or a short one, a four-line blurb, a one-line blurb, multiple authors, a photographer or editor credit—it all goes into the design mix and must be reckoned with.

Note: In this chapter a book's "cover" refers to its cover *design*. Hardcovers and paperbacks have different kinds of physical covers (paper, jacket, case—see chapter 1) which all feature their cover (design).

The Title

For most covers (bestselling authors excepted), the title reigns supreme and must be treated as monarch. The rest of the information—textual and visual—fits itself around this all-important element, with varying levels of preference and importance. Like the cover itself, the title is intended as a beautiful, or at least memorable, distillation of all that lies within. A great title reels you in with its force, poetry, or surprising juxtaposition of words. Hearing the title of a not-yet-designed book sparks ideas in my mind; the words, even the letters themselves, suggest images, layout, type treatment—the first flashes of design.

Short titles pull a design one way. Long titles pull it another. The cover for Dave Eggers's *A Heartbreaking Work of Staggering Genius* is going to need a very different design approach than the cover for Stephen King's *It*. If you are dreaming of a bold, punchy cover, you might reconsider that six-word title that includes the word

Productivity. A lot of words or long words in a title will require smaller or more condensed type and less room for imagery. I'm not trying to tell you what to call your book; just be aware.

The Author's Name

If you are a mere mortal, your name will most likely be of moderate size, most likely in the lower third of a cover. Famous authors, particularly bestselling genre authors, get their names up top or very large, or both. The author's name should be treated with respect, but in most cases it isn't the primary draw, and the design will reflect this. The name can be twinned with the title, sharing color and font (but usually not size), with the subtitle acting as a counterpoint in between the two. It's common to keep an author's name on a single line, but some designs require that it be stacked. The author's credentials or previous notable books, when included, should sit beneath their name, and much smaller.

The Subtitle

The subtitle provides all the relevant information that a poetically evocative title doesn't, beckoning the book browser, "Come closer, let me tell you more." Subtitles provide additional context and explain or expand an idea suggested by the title. They situate a book editorially and signal to the reader that a book is nonfiction or information oriented. They are also increasingly important for search engine optimization and online discovery, which may account for some very long subtitles that seem to cram in the keywords. Subtitles do turn up occasionally on fiction covers, but it's rare.

Adding a subtitle to a cover complicates the design and, to some extent, shifts the focus. Even on a cover with plenty of imagery, adding more words to a cover makes a cover more about the words. The length of the subtitle and where the lines need to break for sense will lead a designer toward different ideas and solutions. A long rambling subtitle may be appropriate, but it will require a different treatment than one that is short and pointed. Differentiating the subtitle from other

The Parts of a Cover

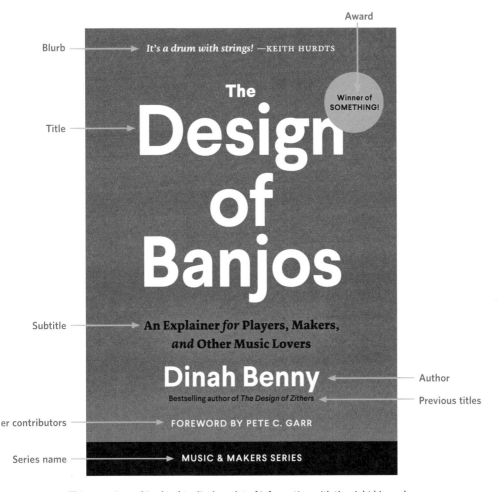

Award

Blurb

Title

Subtitle

er contributors

Series name

It's a drum with strings! —KEITH HURDTS

The

Design
of
Banjos

Winner of
SOMETHING!

An Explainer *for* Players, Makers,
and Other Music Lovers

Dinah Benny

Bestselling author of *The Design of Zithers*

FOREWORD BY PETE C. GARR

MUSIC & MAKERS SERIES

Author

Previous titles

This cover is working hard to display a lot of information with the right hierarchy.

text on the cover, getting it to play nice with images, and making it big enough (but not too big) are additional preoccupations. Titles and subtitles are major design elements, sometimes the *only* design elements (along with the name of the author) on a cover. How they look, what they say, and how they say it command a lot of attention from the viewer and, thus, from the designer.

The Reading Line, Series Line, or Tagline

A funny piece of publishing jargon, the reading line isn't quite a subtitle but isn't that different from one either. In genres that rarely use subtitles, the reading line might provide a crucial piece of clarifying data: "A Novel," "Essays," "Poems." In a series, the reading (or series) line might say "Part III of *The Lord of the Rings*" or "A Jack Reacher Novel." Occasionally, particularly in genre fiction, a reading line might tease the plot: "A city like no other, a story without end." Some people refer to this as a tagline. In nonfiction, reading lines can act as supplemental information, in addition to a subtitle, when the publisher wants to be sure the audience understands all the book has to offer: "With 100 recipes you can make in a microwave!"

Reading lines occupy a funny space for designers as well. Very short phrases can be plainly stated or treated more decoratively. It's not unusual to see "A Novel" integrated into a design in an ornamental way, even when the rest of the text is handled in a more straightforward manner. A longer reading line needs to be differentiated from the subtitle, in which case it might be handled in a "burst" (a colored shape, often a circle, that can be placed in a quiet corner of a cover, or even overlapping part of an image or text; also called a "violator") to make it clear to the reader that it is a distinct piece of information, and to save the cover from line after line after line of straight text.

Blurbs

The question of whether blurbs—praise from reviews or from other authors—are an effective marketing tool or a racket is primarily an editorial debate. For the designer, blurbs are mostly a back-cover element, and when they appear on the front cover, they tend to be short (please!), hyperbolic, and by someone (or some place) whose name pulls some weight. A pithy blurb can be a bright exclamation point on a cover. But blurbs that go on and on (and with credit lines that go on and on) become a real drag on a design, hogging an unjustified amount of visual and psychic space.

Additional Credit Lines

"Foreword by," "Edited by," "Photographs by," "Illustrated by," "Translated by"—there's nothing like setting these small lines of text to underscore how the designer must balance the cover's existence as an object of beauty with its function as a conveyor of information. I work hard to keep this material distinct and legible without letting it encroach on the cover's visual impact.

Distinctions

Important awards or honors won by the book or the author are often proudly announced on the front cover. If you're lucky enough to have a national bestseller or major motion picture tie-in, by all means let us know! Like blurbs, these secondary pieces of text are explicitly sales copy and are usually held at a little distance from the primary design. Many corporate or official book clubs—Oprah's, Jenna's, Reese's—and major literary awards sport a logo they "allow" publishers to include on their covers. These bursts are usually deliberately placed over part of the "existing" design to emphasize their role as an honor that has been bestowed upon the book postpublication.

Images

Oh right, images! Aside from all that text, most covers feature art of one sort or another (I discuss those that don't on page 76). But while the text is provided and prescribed by others, envisioning, finding, choosing (or creating), and manipulating imagery is generally the purview of the designer. Some cover assignments arrive with a suggested image or images, often from the author. Some lucky books warrant the creation of original artwork or a photo shot specifically for the cover, often the conception of the art director. *Most* covers use images that already exist in the world and that the designer must go out and dig up. I will discuss how designers select and handle imagery in more depth later.

The Creative Brief

At a traditional publishing house, folks have been talking and thinking about a book for who knows how long before they begin discussing the cover. They've read a proposal, considered where the book might fit on their list, huddled with the author, agreed to acquire it, read and edited the manuscript, and developed the specs. The editor may have been working with an author for a year, or many years, before the question of cover design comes along.

Depending on where the book is in development, the manuscript may or may not be finished when cover design commences. For fiction and poetry, particularly, the author's voice and writing style will affect how a cover looks, and designers are usually given at least a partial or rough manuscript. For nonfiction, its common to give the designer a chapter or two, to get a sense of the author's voice, and the table of contents, to understand the scope. For visual books, getting-to-know-you often entails looking through a folder of images.

All books come with a creative brief (also called a cover brief or design brief). The "brief" is usually created with input from the entire publishing team—the editor, art director, publisher, marketing team, and author—and allows everyone to focus and agree upon what the book *is* (and, also, what it isn't) and how they envision it in the market. The brief is given to a designer—whether in-house or freelance—at the beginning of a project and, if it's thoughtful and thorough, should launch the designer in a few specific directions.

If you are self-publishing, no one is going to create a cover brief for you. I strongly recommend that you go through the exercise of creating one for yourself. This important preliminary phase will help you understand what you'd like your book cover to do, cutting short a thousand errant ideas, and allowing the designer to embark from a place of knowledge and mutual understanding. Following is the information you'll find in most creative briefs and which I use to orient myself before beginning design.

Cover Copy

Titles and subtitles are hugely impactful to everything about a book—from a marketing perspective to a literary one—and often shift and change during writing and development. As I discussed earlier, every piece of text on the cover affects the cover design. By the time the brief is passed along to the designer, the wording for titles, and everything else on the cover, should be nailed down tight. It would be disingenuous, though, to claim that text never changes midprocess, or even after. It does. (Titles rarely do, but it's not completely unheard of. At that point I ask for more money.) Subtitles get tweaked. Reading lines are added. Maybe an author gets an exciting and unexpected blurb that needs to be tacked on at the last minute. This is the reality for a cover designer. But just know: even a small text change down the road can upset an already set and balanced design.

Specs

The trim size of the book, whether it will be a hardcover (jacketed or not) or paperback, and whether the interior will be printed in color or black ink will be stated in the cover brief. These are the printer's specs. A book's size and shape are economic, editorial, and market factors, largely determined by its genre, function, and cost, and have probably been determined well before design begins. But a book's dimensions are design decisions as well and have a big impact on how the cover design is visualized and executed. If you missed it, see chapter 1 for a more thorough explanation of specs.

Sales Copy or Book Synopsis

Some description of the book is usually included in a creative brief. If you are self-publishing, you will need to write this yourself to give to a designer who most likely will not read your manuscript (in full or at all). A book synopsis is helpful in that it allows the publishing team, or self-publishing author, to highlight what they consider the book's most salient aspects and how they intend to position it.

Audience

Covers are created to appeal to . . . somebody. Who that somebody is might be determined by demographic information (teens, mothers, seniors), subculture (gamers, cooks, hobbyists), or reading history (fans of speculative fiction, devotees of presidential biographies, or everyone who devoured *Twilight*). Defining this group or groups as clearly and specifically as possible will keep the designer on a constructive course. I once worked on a design for a book about cookie decorating. The cover brief stated that the book, because of the author's punk rock approach to icing their cookies, was aimed at millennials and younger readers, not the middle-aged demographic that is often the audience for baking books. Design choices aimed at older folks—from palette to typography to imagery—look very different from the ones aimed at an audience of twenty- or thirty-somethings. Instead of doilies and gingerbread men we showed modern bakeware and sugar skulls.

Comps

Comps is short for *competitive* or *comparable titles*[3]—the group of books that will be next to this one on the bookstore or library shelf or that will come up in a keyword search online. Understanding a book's category is ground zero for the designer, and for everyone on the publishing team. Book genres and categories have their own set of conventions that, even when subverted or reinvented, must be thoroughly understood. Editors think hard about the comps for a book—and how they've sold—before acquiring a new manuscript. Once they've decided to publish a book, the comps help guide decisions regarding price, specs, the marketing campaign, and the cover design.

The cover brief will provide a list of the most relevant and successful comp titles, usually as a group of thumbnails (mini versions of the covers). Authors who are self-publishing should cut and paste these covers onto a document (or digital "board") themselves so they can see them together. What are the common elements? What aspects of color palette, font choice, image style, and layout appear again and again? If the book is in a popular category, you might go to a bookstore to see some of these titles in the flesh. What are their sizes, materials, and feel?

Different kinds of books adhere to norms more strictly than others. Genre fiction and business books are tight-knit and cliquish, and their covers often share many conventions to identify themselves as part of the club. Literary fiction, on the other hand, is broader and more unconventional, rewarding novelty and the pushing of boundaries.

As I work through cover ideas I will often come back to the comps and, quite literally, add my design ideas into that group of thumbnails. Seeing my designs among their fellows—how a reader will also likely first encounter a book—is illuminating. Amid the comps, I can see if my type is too weak, the palette feels tired, or—gasp—the concept has already been used (twice!). Then again, the cover might just beam and I'll be able to see that too.

Design Direction

Ideas for cover design that come from the publishing team, art director, or author will be described in the brief. The direction might be general, "We'd like to emphasize the book's setting in rural Japan," or quite specific, "Please try a type treatment like what was used for *She Said*." Images might be suggested or provided. A specific style, mood, or illustrator might be proposed. There is almost never a suggestion like "Render the scene where Juliet discovers the magic trumpet while the wizard is sleeping under the tree." Most covers—including those of genre fiction—don't portray literal scenes from the book or a catalog of central elements. Covers are distilled representations of the work, not movie trailers.

How an author gets their ideas into the cover brief, and under the nose of the designer, is covered in chapter 7. For now, it's good to know that there is a process for sharing these thoughts, and that it's in the cover brief that those ideas are most likely to be relayed. No one knows a book like its author, and while micromanaging isn't appreciated, ideas about images and approach certainly are. If you are a self-publishing author, you must adopt the role of art director here. What direction would you like this cover to take? How should it be positioned?

Maybe it's obvious, but sometimes really good concepts don't end up as really good designs. Once worked through, a promising direction may not come together as hoped or be as compelling as others that bubble up along the way. The design ideas in the cover brief are the stepping-off point for the designer and rarely exactly where we end up.

Genre

Books don't come with a sticker that says "mystery" or "self-help" or "literary fiction" slapped across their fronts, but they need to get the point across anyway. A cover's first function is to answer the question: What kind of book is this? For most books this means that cover designs stick to established layouts, type treatments, imagery, and color schemes. Fitting in with the crowd is the most reliable way for a book to find its readership. Some genres have a more recognizable set of motifs than others, and a few—notably literary fiction and some kinds of illustrated or design-forward books—reward originality and innovation. Sticking close to conventions doesn't necessarily equal bad or boring design. Within even the most narrowly defined genres, strong designers bring a fresh perspective to familiar formulas. Like a teen at the prom, the best covers will both fit in and stand out.

Nonfiction

Nonfiction is a big, big tent, encompassing everything from *Who Moved My Cheese?* to Thoreau's *Walden*. Appropriately, there are lots of different looks. But whether cover design is buttoned up and traditional or loose and trying new things, its goals are the same: communicate what a book is about and what it's *like*. "It's about corporate management but it's lighthearted." "It's about clowns and it's serious." "It's about nature and it's *very* serious." Titles are the most prominent aspect of most covers and they sometimes tell you what you need to know. If they're more interested in being charming than informative, the subtitle is there to prop them up. Design adds typography (or

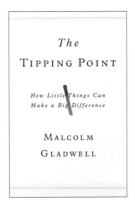 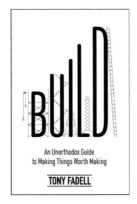 

In the twenty-first century (so far), a white cover screams "nonfiction."

lettering), color, and images to the mix, marrying information with energy, placing the text within a context.

Nonfiction books can be about people, events, and things—which are easily visualized—or primarily about ideas, which aren't. Designing a cover for a book on Frank Sinatra is a whole different project than designing one for a book on being a better boss (or mother, or lover, or person). For the Sinatra book it's clear: I'd be a fool not to put his gorgeous face on the cover (I'm not, and I have). It's not that these books are easy to design—there are a thousand pictures of Frank and a million ways to go with a cover—but when you start with a noun, you at least get the *what* out of the way.

So what to do with books about abstractions—concepts, systems, dynamics, or states of being? What belongs on the cover of a book about problem-solving? (The Rubik's Cube is already taken.) Grief? Mindfulness? Getting ahead in your career? The subjects of many of the most popular kinds of nonfiction don't have an obvious visual referent. Type-only covers are often the solution to this conundrum. Decorative covers, which rely heavily on color and pattern or abstract imagery, work for some categories, less well for others. Some concept-driven nonfiction calls for a concept-driven cover—a visual metaphor that distills the ideas of the text in a quickly grokked but oh-so-clever bite. Sometimes this is an image, sometimes a type treatment, sometimes the type becomes an image of sorts. Tony Fadell's book *Build* features the letters of the title with ladders and scaffolding set around them, as if the word itself is being built. In Yuval Noah Harari's *Sapiens* the dot of the *i* (charmingly called a tittle) is a human fingerprint.

And then there's *The Tipping Point.* The cover for Malcolm Gladwell's 2002 megahit featured a clean white background, traditional typography, and the image of a single unlit match. The formula for this cover—dominant title and small metaphorical image—was so wildly popular that it became the template for concept-driven, non-fiction book covers for years. (I'm not sure we're over it yet.) Concept-driven covers are deceptively hard to pull off. Because they have a clean aesthetic and are mostly type, people may assume they're easy to design—there's barely anything there! In reality, translating big ideas into elegant visual metaphors is quite a task.

Fiction

Covers for fiction tend to be expressive and imaginative, like the stories they wrap themselves around. Titles are often ambiguous or poetic and there's (usually) no subtitle to provide context and clutter up the canvas. Fiction covers may give clues to character, setting, or plot but equally often traffic in symbolism and abstraction. Designers hope to distill an author's voice, ideas, and words in a single evocative frame. Some narrative nonfiction and, particularly, memoir are written (or at least marketed) as "reading like fiction," and their covers are often designed in this mode as well. They may share the feel of fiction in the hopes of communicating "this is an immersive story."

When designing for fiction (or poetry or other narrative work), I sniff through the manuscript like a bloodhound searching for clues— what element of the landscape, scrap of clothing, physical attribute, plot device, symbolic object, or small-but-potent detail can represent, and carry, the emotional weight of the story? And how should it be presented? The lilt and energy of an author's language may suggest visual attitudes, even colors, even type (to those prone to think in those terms). Designer Linda Huang, commenting on her cover design

1969	1992	2020

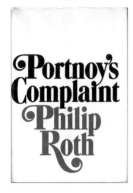  

Expectations of what fiction looks like change over the decades.

for Peter C. Baker's novel *Planes*, said, "I was hoping to convey both elegance and brutality by stylizing the title this way . . ."[4] Can type be brutal? Absolutely.

A lot of fiction is about character, and it can be tempting to show one on the cover. It's a given, though, that you don't want to over-determine what a character looks like. Imagining how a character looks is one of the joys of reading—one that is often corrupted by subsequent movie adaptations. (Oh, Bilbo, how I used to imagine thee!) To avoid this, designers might use parts of the body or figures that are obscured, are in shadow or silhouette, have their heads chopped off, or are viewed from behind. Illustration is more stylized and abstract than photography and, when you can afford it, can be a less specific and more satisfying way to go when putting people (or hobbits) on the cover.

A hardcover book is a luxury object and is sometimes designed like one—nice paper, sewn binding, the most aesthetically oriented cover design. For the covers of these books, particularly, there is an understanding that the designer is *doing* something imaginative (we always are, but . . .) and that that something is related to, but separate from, what the author is doing. Sometimes the hardcover design is reused for the paperback. Other times a design with more clarity or broad appeal (that is, more commercial appeal) is used.

All covers are products of their era and its fashion. Display fonts are as trendy as pop songs. Type-focused covers, photographic covers, covers with figurative illustration, covers with abstraction—styles emerge, get noticed, proliferate, and eventually are replaced by something else. The covers of today are stamped with the characteristics of their era as clearly as those of the 1980s or 1950s were stamped with theirs. The successful covers of successful books are included in creative briefs as comps. Designers not only naturally respond to trends and culture but are explicitly asked to do so.

Trends sometimes veer into stereotypes. Fiction by or about female, Black, Asian, Latino, Arab, queer, and otherwise-othered people is often pinned to their identities through clichéd imagery, color, and type. Writers who are women complain about the repeated use of "woman doing nothing" or "sexy back" as belittling and tired tropes on their covers.[5] A blog post on the website Africa Is a Country once pointed to thirty-six books with African themes all featuring acacia trees and orange skies on those covers: "The covers of most novels 'about Africa' seem to have been designed by someone whose principal idea of the continent comes from The Lion King."[6] Commenting on the trend, the writer Michael Silverberg noted, "Certain books are allowed to stand on their own; others—too often those by African, Muslim, or female authors—are assigned genre stereotypes."[7]

I once designed a cover for a novel about a volatile gay romance set in Sydney, and my first round of covers featured a couple embracing against a lavender background. The type was expressive and the image was used interestingly (I thought) but the author was offended and found it stereotyped. The cover we ended up with, after many rounds, was a quiet painting of an interior—referencing the setting and mood rather than the characters. Focusing cover design on generalized aspects of identity minimizes the breadth of a story and narrows its potential readership. It also, intentionally or not, distances these books from the inner circle of serious literature, which is assumed to address themes of universal consequence. Designers, and everyone involved in positioning a book, should be conscious to avoid relying on used-up (or inaccurate) cover concepts and pigeonholing authors, of any stripe. Every story deserves to be approached anew.

Genre Fiction

Romance, erotica, sci-fi, fantasy, mystery, thriller, horror, and YA are all considered genre fiction: narratives that share specific frameworks or ideas with each other. Fans come to these books specifically for these familiar frameworks, and it is the central job of their covers to identify themselves as members of the club. They have strong visual signals that are repeated on cover after cover.

Successful genre authors are literary stars, and such an author's name on the cover is often the single most important selling point. Inclusion in a series is also an important factor in many genre categories, and calling attention to this feature—"An Alex Cross Mystery"—can be an important element of the cover treatment.

Different genres traffic in different sets of conventions for type style, palette, and imagery. Mysteries and thrillers are famous for their large type, shadowy backgrounds, drips of blood, and bullet holes. Romances are known for embracing couples (yes, still), a light, bright palette, and "feminine" (sorry) type treatments. Covers for fantasy novels are almost always illustrated—there aren't many photographs of orcs available. YA fiction also usually sports illustration and is more likely to show characters on its covers. Other categories have their own customs, and creating covers for any of them requires the designer to have a thorough understanding of their idiom.

This isn't to say that the covers for genre fiction can't look really good and present something new. When the hardcover of *The Girl with the Dragon Tattoo* came out in the US, aside from creating a literary sensation, it drew wide attention for its boundary-pushing cover. The cover designer, Peter Mendelsund, ignored the established conventions of the thriller and went with a wholly different palette (bright and acidic as opposed to the traditional dark and shadowy), imagery (decorative rather than explicitly creepy), and title treatment (playful and relatively restrained). It looked nothing like the other books on the shelf in the thriller section. Why this worked can partially be explained by the huge popularity of the story itself and the hype that preceded it—everyone *knew* it was a thriller; they didn't need the cover to tell them that. Mendelsund reports that he created around fifty ideas for this cover before it was approved and that there was

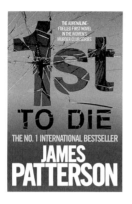  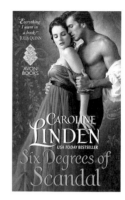

Conventional genre covers (*top row*) and genre-busters (*bottom row*).

pushback from both booksellers and the in-house marketing team.[8] The book went on to sell over three million copies, and the qualities of the design—particularly the way the title breaks and snakes across the cover—are now a treatment that other thrillers imitate (the sincerest form of flattery). The covers for Stephenie Meyer's *Twilight* series and E. L. James's *Fifty Shades of Grey* series were similarly genre-busters that opened up new ideas for how fantasy and erotica, respectively, could be presented.

Type-Only Covers

Many books, in many different categories, go for all-type covers. This approach solves *a lot* of problems. Imagery may feel incompatible with a subject, or the subject may be so abstract that no one can

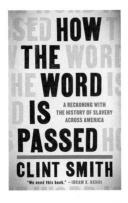 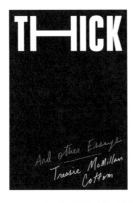 

All-type covers (with a little bit of lettering).

figure out what an appropriate image might be. A book's title may be so strong or clever or rich that leaving it alone on a cover might be the obvious strategy. Dispensing with imagery gives more bandwidth for type to broadcast, and the lack of images has its own allure. Type-only doesn't mean boring or nonvisual. Typography (and lettering) is infinitely malleable, allusive, expressive, and just fun to look at. Used creatively, it can invoke all sorts of moods and feels. Type-only covers often rely heavily on color for emotional cues and sometimes include texture, pattern, or ornament to add visual interest (where pattern and ornament cross over into imagery can be a fine line). Finally, type-only covers save money because no one has to shell out for art.

Illustrated Books

Illustrated books feature images inside, and the covers of illustrated books tend to announce the visual nature of their content. (There's an entire chapter on illustrated books ahead.) They're particularly focused on design and imagery because the books themselves are. While all book covers should look good, these covers must look *good*—a lot of what they're selling is how good they look.

When images are being created specifically for the purposes of the book—as is usually the case for children's picture books or cookbooks, for instance—the design team gets to imagine and commission the cover art, which may be a photograph or an illustration: the exact

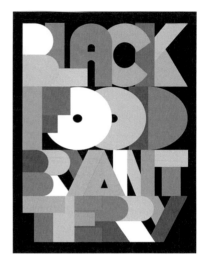

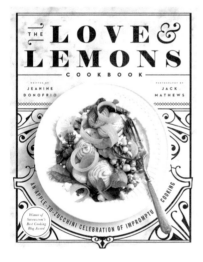

Different kinds of covers for different kinds of illustrated books.

Top left: A "multiples" cover.

Top right: An illustrated book with no image on the cover. Is this title type or image? It's somewhere in between.

Left: An image shot specifically for a cover gives the designer a lot of control over where to place type.

thing we want to show in the exact layout, with the right details, perspective, and color palette. The possibilities! The pressure! Designers are always (well, usually) deciding *what* will end up on the cover, but when commissioning the cover image we get to stage-manage everything, including the space: "Leave exactly this much room for the title. Right here."

Not all illustrated books have commissioned art. Some are collections of preexisting images—a book of Monet's *Water Lilies*, a collection of vintage photographs. With a lot of images at hand, which one gets the starring role? Which is the most representative, the most eye-catching, the most appropriately sized and shaped for the cover? How images act on a cover is different from how they act otherwise, and what makes a good cover image is often surprising to editors and authors. The best cover art holds the space, sits comfortably with type, and communicates immediately. Whether or not it features a person, it needs to look the viewer in the eye.

It's not uncommon for the publishing team to ask for a cover with multiple images when they want to show the range of information covered in a book or when they can't decide on which image is "the one." The "multiples," or collaged, cover can equalize content—if a book presents the stories of a group of different people and the author doesn't want to favor one subject over the rest, for instance—and it can announce: "Look at everything you're going to learn from this book!" These covers may seem a snap from the editorial side—just put every-thing on there!—but are tricky to handle from the design side. Images must be unified in sensibility, if not also color and approach, or the cover will be a mishmash. A grid can be pleasing, but also a snooze. A looser placement of images can easily become chaotic. Titles and sub-titles will usually require a lot of space, a place for viewers to focus. And the trim size needs to be large enough to accommodate all those images and the type. You can understand why designers sometimes groan when the multiples idea is suggested. How can a series of lit-tle squares ever hope to have the impact of the perfect single image? And how can I get a bunch of different images to play nicely together? Still, these covers can work. If the images are right and the space is sufficient (and the designer is good), multiples covers can be strong, elegant, or fun.

After the past forty years of publishers' stubborn conviction that cookbooks *must* show food on the cover, there is a 2020s trend toward type-only (or illustrated) cookbook covers. It's a bold move to go for a type-only approach for *any* book that is filled with images, but it's the subversion of expectations that, sometimes, makes this approach effective. That said, most publishers aren't in the game of subverting market expectations. It can be exceedingly hard to get a green light on a type-focused cover for any illustrated book. The ones that succeed are notable.

Craft

Cover design is graphic design, a commercial art form (interested in both aesthetics and sales), a craft. Like every craft, technique is at its core. Experience and vision bring it to life. Covers created by nondesigners—and in the Wild West of self-publishing they're everywhere—clearly announce this fact. They commit the same sins again and again: poor hierarchy, poor use of fonts (or use of poor fonts, or both), too many colors, not enough negative space, trite imagery, and a heap of drop shadows. Professional designers know how to deploy space, what makes type look polished and read well, and how different kinds of images can be used, cropped, and placed for maximum effect. They have learned the elements of craft that make cover designs work.

The Rectangle

Front cover design is all about that rectangle. While it's true that design can wrap around at least one side—the spine—and, in some cases two—if there are flaps—a simple rectangle is how most people first see a cover, particularly online, and it's where I begin when designing. On a standard 6 × 9–inch hardcover, horizontal space is at a premium, vertically oriented images fit most comfortably, and titles, unless they're very short, must be stacked. A landscape-oriented book, by contrast, offers a vast horizontal field for type and imagery. Long words or even a long title might fit all on one line.

Every element within the frame of the cover is in relationship to the book's trim, or edges, whether it likes it or not. Images or words might sidle alongside an edge, maintain a respectful distance from it, be centered (vertically or horizontally), or run right on off the page. "Bleeding" images off the edge is a common technique (see page 143), allowing the designer to dramatically crop images and suggest continuity with a world beyond the frame.

Placing elements close to an edge (or to each other) creates visual tension, and designers use this tension, deliberately, all the time. But when elements are unintentionally placed too close to edges (or each other), it creates discomfort. I generally don't want tension between, say, the author's name and the bottom edge of a cover. Elements usually need their elbow room, including keeping text comfortably away from edges.

Hierarchy and Balance

There's an order of importance when it comes to the elements on a cover, and I want to be sure the reader is keyed into it, looking first at the title, next at the subtitle, and so on down the line until they get to the title of the book written by the person who has supplied the blurb. Most elements of a cover should feel related, sharing traits like font and color. The pieces that stand out—usually the title, sometimes other things—will do so by broadcasting their difference. Those elements are set bigger or bolder or in a different color or in a different font altogether, drawing the eye.

Along with establishing hierarchy, designers work to keep a cover in balance from top to bottom and side to side. Every element carries weight, and its size, boldness, and color determine how "heavy" or "light" something feels. The title at the top is often mirrored at the bottom by the author's name. Balancing the subtitle against the title and all the other pieces of information requires relentless fine-tuning, turning the knobs of color and size and placement so each element relates to the others just so.

You know what else carries weight? Empty space. A big title can be balanced by a much smaller author's name, if those smaller words have lots of space around them. The term *negative space* might seem like a pretentious way to describe the places where things aren't, but it's as important as anything you can actually see on the cover, the power behind the throne. Now, some designs are chockful of stuff and others are more spare. It's not that all designs need a lot of empty space. Rather, *where* there's space and how much of it are intentional decisions used to create structure, legibility, hierarchy, balance, and drama.

Sometimes after I've spent a lot of time getting my cover to feel locked in—each element inhabiting the appropriate amount of space and presence—the art director up and tells me that the subtitle is changing or we're adding a blurb. Groan. A changed subtitle may now be shorter or longer, which gives it a different presence on the cover, which means the size may need to be bumped up or reduced, which puts it in a different relationship to the author's name and the title, so these elements need to shift as well. There are very few changes that won't send ripples through the pond.

Color

Color can be a unifier or an agent of chaos. It's a strong communicator of emotion and ambiance and, as such, a powerful tool for a designer. A cover never uses just a single color; the term *palette* refers to the set of colors used in any design (black and white, for instance, is a palette).

Different colors evoke different moods—think of how red feels as opposed to pink—and palettes do too. Shades of a single tone (different variations of blue, for instance) can feel cohesive, or subdued, while a group of contrasting tones (blues next to oranges) might feel punchy or just busy. While designing I will often look at a single layout in a variety of palettes: What if the cover was in a range of greens and golds? How about that same cover but in all grays? Purples and blues? Oranges and yellows?

Certain genres favor certain color palettes—thrillers and mysteries are usually full of dark blues, bloody reds, and blacks. Books on mindfulness are often in gentle neutrals or pastels. Crisp white backgrounds are thought to be natty on business books but discouraged for novels (it makes them look too much like business books). Regardless of whether I end up with a sunset of reds and oranges or a seascape of blues and grays, I always aim for a limited palette. For most covers, keeping the set of colors to a smallish group creates a more cohesive and pleasing design and allows the viewer to focus. Even for a book about rainbow unicorns, I would be highly aware of my color palette and keep it under tight control.

Type

On a book cover, type is the star of the show, grabbing most of the attention and, in large part, establishing the feel of the design. As I discussed in the last chapter, typefaces have sensibility and personality and come with all sorts of associations that designers exploit to communicate with an audience. If I'm going for serious and literary, that will lead me toward certain kinds of fonts; strong and punchy will lead me in a different direction; quirky and intimate in yet another. I have a vast library in my head of font styles and categories and over five thousand fonts on my computer, painstakingly organized and cross-referenced for this very process.

Designing the title type for *The Great Gatsby*, I might look through my font folders labeled "art deco," and "classic" and then consider some in my folders labeled "geometric" and "decorative." I might spend a half hour comparing the uppercase *G* in a dozen different typefaces. The differences between fonts might seem subtle, but line twenty *Gatsbys* up together and the variations become quite apparent. Seeing a title expressed in a particular font often helps me to better understand what it is that I wanted to express in the first place.

GATSBY   GATSBY
GATSBY   GATSBY
GATSBY   GATSBY
GATSBY   **GATSBY**
GATSBY   GATSBY
GATSBY   GATSBY

But getting type to work on a cover isn't as simple as picking the right font. Am I going to set the title in all caps, title case, or, less frequently, all lowercase? How many lines should it be broken into, and where should the breaks be? This is an important design *and* legibility issue—where the title breaks helps the reader understand the cadence

The GREAT
GATSBY
F. SCOTT FITZGERALD

F. SCOTT
FITZGERALD

THE GREAT
GATSBY

The
Great
Gatsby

F. Scott
Fitzgerald

The text says the same thing, but in different tones of voice.

and emphasis of the title as well as playing a big role in the overall layout of the cover. Should articles and prepositions be set differently—say, in italics or at a smaller size? Should the subtitle and author's name be in the same font as the title or something contrasting? If contrasting, *how* contrasting (and in what ways)? I'm not just looking for an appropriate typeface but also figuring out how to use it with the right energy.

Cover type is subject to the same laws that all type lives by, but it's larger and more public. While I attend lovingly to the type on the inside of a book (see the next chapter), on the cover I'm a real control freak. I literally assess the space between every single letter to make sure it looks even and natural (unless I'm deliberately going for erratic and odd). As with the color palette, keeping the number of fonts I use on a cover *very* limited helps it feel orderly and unified.

Hand Lettering

Hand lettering is the love child of typography and illustration; the presentation of text that is drawn or painted (if it is drawn or painted on a computer, that is still "hand lettering"). It isn't a font. In a font, each letter will appear the same every time it is used. Every capital G will look identical. But every shape and letter in text that is hand lettered is unique, every time. With its potential for highly expressive and bespoke treatment of words, hand lettering is a natural fit for (some kinds of) book covers and is widely employed. Just like any form of drawing or painting, hand lettering can be tight or loose, very precise or wildly sloppy (but should always be legible!).

Hand lettering has been used on book covers for one hundred years or more but the current trend of highly expressive lettering can be arguably traced to the publication of a single book: Jonathan Safran Foer's 2002 debut novel, *Everything Is Illuminated*, with cover design by Jon Gray (known professionally as gray318). The original cover features white hand lettering against a black background (there are no colors on the jacket but black and white), the letters undulating across the rectangle, uneven, loose, and bursting at the seams. The entire cover is lettered—title, author, and fawning blurb— and there is no other imagery. The lettering is the imagery *and* the text and carries the entire emotional load. (One more touch: the barcode is integrated into the front cover design, an audacious move that I'm not sure I've ever seen repeated.) The

Barcode!

huge success of the book and the high visibility of the cover may have jumpstarted the fashion for using expressive hand lettering on fiction and nonfiction titles that still abides twenty years later. Look around the bookstore and you'll see it everywhere.

Art

Designers use art in different ways for different books, of course. Figuring out what kind of image makes sense for each title is a critical aspect of cover design. A good cover image will have emotional and visual impact—grabbing a reader's attention and pulling them in. It should be appealing, relevant, and resonant and provide ample space for all necessary text. All kinds of images end up on book covers: photography; line art, fine art, and found art; abstractions, ephemera, textures, patterns, doodles, and icons.

Photographs—either contemporary or historical—are an immediate way to communicate subject matter. They're also abundantly available and, in many cases, quite affordable (or, if in the public domain, even free). They make sense for books with small design budgets, which is most books, and are used on all kinds of books in all kinds of ways. "Found" and non-art imagery like signage, packaging, newspaper clippings, old postcards, the covers of old books, and family photos are referential, familiar, and emotive—a natural fit for fiction and narrative nonfiction. Fine art, on the other hand, is erudite and may make a book seem that way too. Poetry collections and scholarly works often reproduce fine art on their covers. Illustration is particularly suited to cover design, being flexible and imaginative—just like the text inside—and allowing the depiction of people, places, and things that don't actually exist in the world. Fantasy and sci-fi, young adult fiction, and children's books nearly always employ illustration on their covers.

Art can come from anywhere—stock image sites, libraries, museums, historical societies, personal collections, artist's websites, or the author's mother's attic. The larger the art budget, the more freedom the designer has to search far and wide for images—opening up access to the higher-end image databases (and their prettier pictures) and to original art. Art directors sometimes commission art from illustrators or other artists or shoot photography specifically for a cover design. (Designer and illustrator are two different jobs with different skill sets. If an original piece of art is required for a cover, it will most likely be created by someone other than the designer.)

All images are manipulated to some degree—from the fairly straightforward adjustment of size or tone to full-on disfigurement. Working with mediocre stock imagery—a common predicament—often requires a skilled array of transformative techniques to take a trite, or even ugly, image and get it ready for its big moment. Images are blown up, cut up, and degraded; juxtaposed or entangled with type; collaged and layered with other images; recolored and desaturated; rotated; turned upside down and backward.

For a story that takes place in the Colorado Rockies, for example, I might find a stock photograph of a snowy mountainside. Out of the box, it probably looks pretty generic. I might enhance it by punching up or subduing its colors, adding a subtle grain to give it some texture, cropping it for stronger impact, and pasting in a little cabin from another image entirely. I could also create a dramatic tear through the center to express emotional disjuncture, double expose a face on top to represent the narrator, turn the sky bright pink to suggest a bizarre turn of events, or turn the whole image on its side (or upside down) for a surprising visual and emotional jolt. I could blur it or smudge it, scribble on it, cut it up, or hide parts of it with the parts of other images.

Designers do all sorts of things with the art they find or are given. The *treatment* of an image is as much a part of its latent meaning and emotional punch as its content. That said, when working with fine art that isn't in the public domain, artists and estates must always give permission for use and for any adjustment of the artwork, including, sometimes, cropping and type overlays.

Type and Image

Some images take up the whole cover (that's called a full bleed), some use half or part of the cover (a partial bleed). Some are inset like a frame within a frame. A spot image is cut out from its background and can be used anywhere it fits. (See page 143 for examples.) Where might it fit? Does the image determine where the text can go, or does the text (and the amount of text) determine what kind of image will work? Which comes first, the chicken or the egg? Exactly.

Some cover designs are splashed from edge to edge with imagery, and type is tucked or entwined or fit within it. Other designs do the opposite—sprinkling imagery onto or between a bold treatment of type. I sometimes let my type and image flirt: when image and text acknowledge each other, even a little bit (by, say, an image overlaying a corner of the type or type overlaying the corner of an image), it can bring energy and unity to a design.

Type and Images

There are a million ways type can interact with an image.

But much of the time images and type keep to themselves. The text must be read! Color boxes, bands, and other shapes can be a clean, calm place for type (this element is called the holding shape) and keep it highly visible and legible. It isn't uncommon for type to inhabit one part of a cover and the image the other part, never the two shall meet. Even on covers where type is sitting over part of an image, it will almost always be corralled into a quiet area, steering clear of busy or "important" parts of the picture. Photographs that work well for covers are often almost completely empty in their upper half to leave a quiet space for the title. I'll shift, resize, rebreak, Photoshop, and otherwise adjust both image and type—tweak, tweak, tweak—as I bring them together in a harmonic equipoise of beauty and legibility.

Texture

The use of texture is a designer's stealth technique—routinely deployed but rarely noticed, subtle but significant, bringing cohesion, depth, and credibility to a design. Texture might be used literally—I can place a wood grain as a background on a cookbook cover to suggest a cutting board or stick an aged paper texture underneath type to signal "historical." More commonly I will use textures quietly—adding a little graininess, a soft marbling, some modest distressing, or muted patterning below or within a design.

To what end? As I've mentioned, stock images can be a little cheesy. Deslicking digital imagery by adding grain, natural variation, and subtle degradation can make them feel analog, authentic, and, well, more soulful. Texture can also differentiate objects, suggest dimension, and bring a tactile quality to a cover, working against its natural (and actual) flatness. I keep a large library of textures—concrete, sand, metal, wood, film grain, watercolor washes and ink splotches, cardboards, various fabrics and papers, and geometric and organic patterns—that I sneak into designs again and again. They keep things interesting and can bring a "finish" to the design like grinding fresh pepper over your soup. Not all covers need additional texture; some images are busy enough as they are or are *trying* to appear slick and digital. Some designs revel in their "flatness" and look great that way.

Printing Effects

Good-looking designs can become great-looking covers with the thoughtful use of printing effects, as discussed in chapter 1. Spot gloss, embossed paper, spot colors, and debossed areas of type or image are fairly common, and relatively affordable, extras that can reinforce the graphic ideas of a cover and bring to it a satisfying tactile quality. But because specs are decided early and the cover design may be happening months or years later, designers can find themselves faced with specs that don't make sense with, or limit, the design as it develops. I often find myself arguing for the value of added production elements in the face of a budget that was set long ago. Editors, worrying over costs, reasonably see these choices as highly optional and find it easy to say no. I often see the use of effects as the full realization of a design idea, the difference between "meh" and "wow!" (This is true on covers and in all aspects of the book's physical form. The lack of design input during the discussion of production specs is a missed opportunity for everyone.) If a publisher shifts to digital printing after an initial offset print run (it happens), that can mean that special effects used in the first printing aren't present in later editions of the book.

Process

Every designer will have a different process for harnessing the elements of craft, of course. For me, once the project has been offered and accepted, the brief received, the comps studied, and the manuscript read (or parts of it), I will start by creating a new file in my design application, InDesign, the exact size of the future cover. "Oh! Look at that!" Is it slim or broad, strongly vertical or nearly square? The size and proportion of that rectangle is the first element of the design and, even sitting empty on the screen, it sparks ideas and suggests design directions.

Then, depending on the kind of book I'm working on and the images or direction I've been given, I start the process of "sketching." Sketching might evoke images of pencil and paper, but sketching can take many forms, and for me, usually, it looks more like dropping images and text onto that blank rectangle on my screen. If the publisher has provided images, I'll study the group and see what feels strong, graphic, appealing, dynamic, and representative, and has room for type. Plop, plop, plop—I'll drop a bunch of those images into my file.

If the brief comes without its own images, I begin the hunt for images that feel strong, graphic, appealing, dynamic, and representative, and have room for type. Let's say I'm designing the book *The Design of Banjos*. The cover brief suggested—what? A photograph of a banjo on the cover! I'll take a look around (mostly online, but not exclusively). What kind of banjo images are out there? How to choose? Images I find iconic, novel, particularly graphic, or beautifully shot or drawn or painted will draw my attention. Plop, plop, plop. How do they sit in the frame? It's often clear as soon as an image lands inside my rectangle that it's not going to work: too cliché, too busy, the wrong scale or proportion for the cover, no room for type. Click, delete.

Searching for images is a time-consuming, and sometimes tedious, process. Stock-photo sites and image databases, Pinterest, Google Image, illustrators' sites, photographers' sites, the Library of Congress, I look and look and look. And I'll usually repeat this process of looking for images one, two, three more times throughout the design process as I throw out early picks and gain a sharper idea of what I'm looking for. Providing a designer with an image or images from the outset—assuming they're strong, appropriate, and workable—can cut the project hours enormously. (All images used for a final cover must be appropriately licensed, credited, and paid for, of course.)

At some point I'll move on from the hunt and will start pushing images around the rectangle—placing, moving, cropping, enlarging, or bleeding them—and set some initial type on top. Is there room? No? What else could I do with the type? A box? A band? Maybe I'll set the title inside the shape of the banjo. What if the cover was *mostly* type with the image claiming a minority stake? Maybe I'll silhouette the image—which means cutting out the background—and put a different kind of background behind it. That banjo was leaning against a wall, now it's leaning against the railing of a front porch. Or floating in the clouds. Does the type fit now? What should that type look like? Classic and authoritative, clean and modern, old-timey? Would hand lettering enhance this cover? What kind of hand lettering? Does any of this feel right? Let me look at the cover brief again.

Once I've spent some time with suggested directions, I'll take my own counsel—what else could happen here? A drawing might feel special and more literary than a photo. A watercolor could be charming and give me a lot of flexibility with composition. What if I show the banjo maker rather than the instrument? Or an abstract illustration that just suggests the strings or the tuning pegs? Could I convince the publisher to do a die cut? Foil stamping? Do I really even need to show a banjo?

Typically I'll end up with three or four covers that I present to the art director: a mix of the ideas from the brief and ones that bubbled up as I worked with the material. Offering a variety of genuinely different takes allows the publishing team to see how different moods and modes play out and clarify what is working and feels like a fit. I take care to remember that they have not spent the last three weeks at my elbow, watching as I work through dozens of different approaches. They don't know all the many roads I've started down, and what I've tried hard to make work but ultimately rejected as a dead end. In an email I will describe my thinking and what I believe each approach accomplishes. If I haven't followed a lead suggested in the brief, I explain why not. Ideas that look good in theory don't always pan out visually. Some art is beloved but ends up limp or busy on a cover. Sometimes I can't find or afford the imagery that would make a concept work. Sometimes I'm not technically skilled enough to make a concept work. Sometimes the amount of words needed to fit on a cover, or even the specifics of what those words are, will make a plausible idea untenable. I've learned never to submit, even at early stages, a cover that I really dislike and couldn't live with. Murphy's Law tells us that's always the one that will be chosen.

Sending in cover ideas isn't the end of the process. Not by a long shot. Other people will review, comment, and suggest. Often many colors, typefaces, or additional concepts will be tried. Where a cover ends up may be close to where it began or in a different universe. I don't adore the final version of every cover I design, and sometimes I'm really disappointed. See chapter 7 for more about the long and winding road that covers must travel before arriving at that stamp of "final approval."

The Online Cover

Amazon has recalibrated so many aspects of our lives that it's shocking to remember that it began as a bookstore. Before it displaced shopping malls, big-box retailers, and "Main Street," Amazon disrupted the publishing industry in massive ways, and continues to do so.[9] And while the books sold at Amazon, and everywhere online, are the same ones you find at your local indie, the way they look—in all those places—is a product of Amazon's monumental influence.

At the beginning of this chapter, I mentioned how book covers call to us from the display tables and windows of bookstores. The reality is that many of us first encounter the books we buy online. And whether it's in an Instagram ad, reader forums, author or publisher websites, newspaper or media reviews, or our local indie's site, we more often than not first see a book cover as an inch-high rectangle on our screens. Naturally, publishers and designers have adapted to this paradigm. Where, in the 1990s, the marketing team might have asked the design team for a cover you could read from across the room, they now ask for a cover that looks great at 300 × 400 pixels.

If book covers were going to be viewed only tiny on the screen, we would design them that way. The trouble for designers is that covers need to look good in miniature on the screen *and* full sized in your hands. How to create a cover that can scale is an added challenge for the twenty-first-century cover designer. Practically speaking, this has led to certain design solutions that work well in both contexts: big type, bright colors, and highly graphic and legible artwork. There's nothing wrong with this; in fact I love this kind of cover. But it's not the *only* kind of cover, and it doesn't fit every kind of book. Small(er) type, texture, subtle or detailed imagery, and physical materials don't read well, or at all, small on the screen, and it's hard to get these kinds of covers past the folks upstairs at the publishing house.

In 2009, the designer Isaac Tobin suggested that the presence of ebooks and the increasing shift to buying and marketing books online would eventually cause some reevaluation of cover design. In an interview on the book-focused blog *The Casual Optimist*, he said, "I would speculate that cover design is going to get less focused on the cover itself and more on what you might call book identity systems. As books are increasingly sold in multiple formats and for different devices, we'll have to transition away from designing objects to designing open ended systems."[10]

In the early 2010s, there was a movement among some publishers to create two covers for each title—a primary cover that appeared printed on the book and a related cover optimized for viewing online. These days, some covers get cool animated versions—elements appearing and disappearing, sliding down, whooshing in, before they congeal into the final cover design—the better to capture attention when scrolling by on Instagram. This expansion of what covers can look like and do is appropriate and exciting. But physical books will always need their forever wrappers. For all the innovation possible with digital display, it is the old paper-and-ink version that we'll discover on a dusty shelf in a rented vacation house twenty years from now. To design books with only the selling capacity of the online version in mind is too narrow a vision.

The Rest of the Cover

One of the unique pleasures of book cover design is that it gets to both use and abuse its frame. The front cover is a two-dimensional canvas but the *book* is a three-dimensional object. The designer can play against those four front cover edges *and*, if desired, wrap the design around the spine and on to the back cover (or, on the opposing edge, the flaps). What fun! In hand, a reader engages with a book in this way too, flipping it over to read the back, opening to the front flap, turning the book in their hands, and—purposefully or not—following the design around the object.

The Spine

I absolutely love the spines of books—I consider them old friends on my bookcase, and I adore designing them. That narrow shape—so iconic—is just begging for a strong design to announce its identity to the world. A book's spine, once it's been bought and read, becomes a book's most familiar feature. The writer and designer Derek Birdsall called the spine "a visual database" that reminds us of "the cover—and the contents—of a book."[11] It's only a select group of books that are displayed "face out" at a bookstore. Most books will be encountered by readers spine-first and a dynamic spine design will draw their eyes.

The spine should, of course, echo the front cover design, if not continue it literally. Type treatment for the title (and author) will not necessarily be identical to its treatment on the front (it's a different space with different needs) but will usually share the same typeface and palette. Design elements that had seemed to be dynamically

The Parts of a Jacket

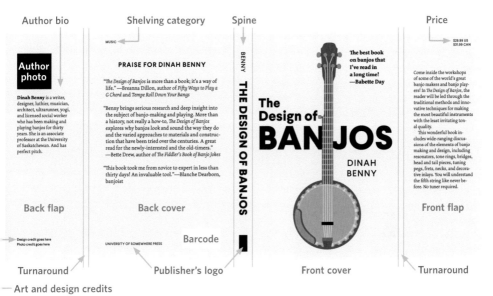

Author bio · Shelving category · Spine · Price · Back flap · Back cover · Barcode · Front flap · Turnaround · Publisher's logo · Front cover · Turnaround · Art and design credits

MUSIC

PRAISE FOR DINAH BENNY

"The Design of Banjos is more than a book; it's a way of life." —Breanna Dillon, author of *Fifty Ways to Play a G Chord* and *Tempe Roll Down Your Bangs*

"Benny brings serious research and deep insight into the subject of banjo-making and playing. More than a history, not really a how-to, The Design of Banjos explores why banjos look and sound the way they do and the varied approaches to materials and construction that have been tried over the centuries. A great read for the newly-interested and the old-timers." —Bette Drew, author of *The Fiddler's Book of Banjo Jokes*

"This book took me from novice to expert in less than thirty days! An invaluable tool." —Blanche Dearborn, banjoist

UNIVERSITY OF SOMEWHERE PRESS

Author photo

Dinah Benny is a writer, designer, luthier, musician, architect, ultrarunner, yogi, and licensed social worker who has been making and playing banjos for thirty years. She is an associate professor at the University of Saskatchewan. And has perfect pitch.

Design credit goes here
Photo credit goes here

BENNY
THE DESIGN OF BANJOS

The Design of **BANJOS**
DINAH BENNY

The best book on banjos that I've read in a long time! —Babette Day

Come inside the workshops of some of the world's great banjo makers and banjo players! In *The Design of Banjos*, the reader will be led through the traditional methods and innovative techniques for making the most beautiful instruments with the least irritating tonal quality.

This wonderful book includes wide-ranging discussions of the elements of banjo making and design, including resonators, tone rings, bridges, head and tail pieces, tuning pegs, frets, necks, and decorative inlays. You will understand the fifth string like never before. No tuner required.

$28.99 US
$31.99 CAN

Designers work on jackets (and editors and authors review them) on a flat plane, not as the three-dimensional objects they will become. This is how they appear on a screen.

cropped on the front cover can be revealed to, in fact, continue onto the spine (and possibly around to the back). A spine is also a space of its own where elements of the cover design can be expanded or elaborated (or knowingly subverted). The fact is, a book's spine becomes its "face" and primary identifier once it's tucked onto the shelf.

Title text can be displayed horizontally and stacked down a spine, but there has to be a lucky confluence of events for this to occur (basically: short title, wide spine). In older books, you will sometimes see long words in a title broken by a hyphen in order to allow for them to be displayed horizontally. (Whenever I encounter this, I cheer. I'm a devoted advocate of the hyphen, as you'll see in the chapter 4.) For most contemporary books, spine text appears "sideways" down the spine. In the US, the UK, and Canada, the text goes top to bottom, facing the back cover. In other parts of the world, text goes the other way, facing the front.

The Back Cover

Has anyone ever sung the praises of a back-cover design? They should. The back cover works hard—and so does its designer—to contain and present a lot of information, clearly and with style. Jacketed books, which have flaps, have a little leeway. For paperbacks and unjacketed hardcovers, the back cover has to manage it all: a headline; a summary of the book's plot or contents (this is referred to as sales copy); a parade of blurbs and their attributions (sometimes longer than the blurb itself); and the author's bio, sometimes with a photo. At some publishing houses the text on the back of the book is referred to as the back ad. The bottom few inches is reserved for the publisher's logo, design and illustration credits, and the (often disparaged) bar code. Tucked in somewhere—usually the top corner, sometimes over the barcode—is the shelving category: the name of the section of the store where the publisher would like the bookseller to shelve the book (honestly, bookstores use this; it's not always self-evident). This is a lot of text to deal with in a small area. All of it is important—but not equally important—and the reader should always know what they're looking at. A blurb should not be mistaken for sales copy.

The whole program should be in sync with the front cover and spine design. There can be an urge to dress up the back cover—"um, can there be more *design* here?" If there's room, and it makes sense, I go for it. (But, let's be honest, there's rarely room.) Design elements generally should appear around the text, not beneath it, where they will compromise legibility. If there's a lot of information to pack in, a simple and straightforward design is completely appropriate. One final note: when looking at smallish text, as is often the case on back covers, color matters. Colored text over a colored background can make reading hard. I always make choices (about color and everything else) with legibility as my priority.

The Foredge and Flaps

The way the foredge (or far edge or right-hand edge) functions depends on the kind of book. When designing for paperbacks (which can have flaps but usually don't), the cover design stops dead at the right-hand edge—that's all there is, there ain't no more. I really like this clean break. Whether I'm creating a centered design or one where elements bleed, that trimmed edge creates a nice strong boundary to work with and against.

For unjacketed hardcovers, the printed paper (or cloth) that covers the book boards rolls around the foredge and underneath the endpaper, carrying the design along with it. Rather than a hard stop, there's a curling away. This area, about ¼ inch wide, is called the turnaround, or board wrap. Because there is no exact edge, the frame (and therefore the center of the frame) is just a little more ambiguous. Designers tend to be meticulous. This ¼ inch of uncertainty kind of drives me crazy.

If a book has a jacket, the design can continue right past the foredge and onto the front flap (where it could, in a certain kind of book, engage with a second design tableau on the endpapers). This allows some designs to really shine—it may not be completely clear where the covers end and the flaps begin, and the design can stretch long arms across the entire jacket. Other designs will benefit from the flap acting as a strong boundary, creating that energy and tension along the foredge, often through a strong shift in color. The front flap (almost always) carries the sales copy and often the shelving category and price. The back flap usually has the author photo and bio, design and illustration credits, and sometime the publisher's logo and info. With flaps carrying some of the textual load, the back covers, for jacketed books, have a little more breathing room for design elements and their roll call of adoring blurbs.

• • •

In some of the larger publishing houses, one designer creates the front cover design and another, often more junior, designer works on the rest of the cover. At these houses, a third designer may be attending to the interior design and typesetting. This assembly-line workflow may make business sense but isn't always satisfying. Regardless of who works on what piece, a polished design should be in tune across the entirety of the cover and all the elements inside.

Chapter 4

Inside the Book

Covers get all the love, but inside the book is where a reader actually spends their time. What's it like in there? Lots of words. But the words don't appear in an undifferentiated block or stream. They're grouped together or meted out, aligned, spaced, styled, and manicured. Without this shaping it's nearly impossible to know what's what. Authors and editors understand this intuitively—even within a Word doc, you set your chapter titles larger, your headings bolder, and add a half dozen hard returns between sections to express structure. This is what book designers do too, but with better tools and a lot more control and finesse.

When I tell people that I design book interiors, many look at me like, "Huh?" A book page is so familiar, and seemingly so straightforward, there may not seem much for a designer to do. But a lot of thinking goes into even the most basic page of text. The work is labor-intensive, fussy, hidden, and yet transformative. Again and again I hear authors delighted at seeing the loosely organized jumble of their Word document reborn as the tightly controlled, stylish form of a considered layout. Authors guide their readers through a book with language. Designers use space and typography. When this is done well, the mechanics of the writing and the design virtually disappear. The hands turn the pages, but the mind is elsewhere, slaying dragons.

The Spread

All books begin on a right-hand page (the recto) and end on a left-hand page (the verso). Since the first page of a book is page 1, and this is a right-hand page, right-hand pages throughout a book are always odd-numbered. When a book is lying open so you can see both the recto and verso at the same time, this is called a spread (or sometimes the redundant "double-page spread" or "full spread"). Designers think and work in spreads. Unlike writers and editors, who scroll through their word processing programs in a single endless flow, designers of print books are always envisioning them the way the reader will ultimately see it—two facing pages at a time.

The left-hand and right-hand pages of a spread are an intimate couple, and a designer works hard to keep them happily married. The pages are reflections of each other, not copies. Text isn't equal distance from the left edge but from the *outside* edge—the left side for a left-hand page and the right side for a right-hand page. We say outside and inside (or outer and inner), not right and left, when referring to margins.

As in many relationships, one partner has a little more pull than the other. In a book, the right-hand (recto) page has higher status. Books open to a recto, and the title page and most important dividers in a book—including the first text page and, sometimes, all of the chapter openers—are placed on this dominant side. There is a superstition among some in publishing that a recto page should never be left blank. Blank verso pages are allowed.

Front Matter

Books are wildly different from each other, but they generally begin and end the same way.

All the business at the beginning of a book is called the front matter. It follows a relatively standard sequence—title page, copyright page, table of contents—and, one might think, is a pretty routine affair. Not from a design perspective. The front matter is the entryway into a book, the reader's second encounter (after the cover design) with its tone and sensibility. Bold, playful, unconventional, artsy, casually elegant, or highly formal—the front matter welcomes the reader, reinforces the mood of the cover, and establishes the interior pacing and style. The title pages and table of contents might be the most graphic and flexible elements in a text-driven book, an early moment to develop a personality before full pages of type take over the visual landscape (those have a personality too, but it's more subtle).

Front Matter

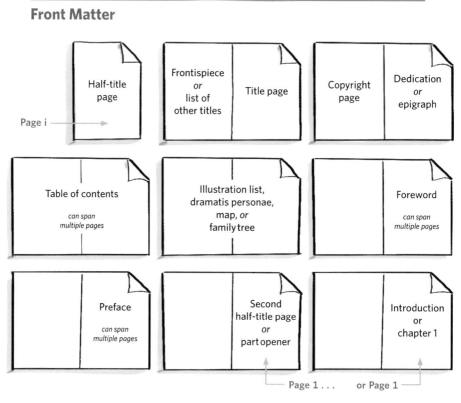

This is a standard sequence for front matter, although different books may require somewhat different solutions.

The front matter is often paginated with roman numerals so that the "official" beginning of the text can start on page 1 (arabic numeral). This dual numbering system saves any late-breaking additions to the front matter—"Michelle Obama agreed to write a foreword!"—from repaginating the entire book, causing an indexing and cross-referencing nightmare. Same is true for later editions and reissues that may have additional or different front matter. Page numbers should not make an appearance until after the table of contents anyway—you never print the page number on, say, the copyright page. Because page 1 can occur ten or twenty pages into a book, don't trust the page number on the last page of a book to be an accurate reflection of the actual page count.

Covers are often designed and approved before interior design begins, and the ideas set forth on the cover, in concert with the specifics of the text, are a good launching pad for the way design plays out inside. One of the simplest and most obvious ways to establish synchronicity between cover and interior is in the front matter. Creating a title page that reflects the spirit, if not the exact layout, of the cover is a basic way of telling the reader: yes, this inside belongs with this outside. This may seem elementary, but grab a couple of novels off your shelf. It isn't at all uncommon for the cover to take one approach and then, when you open the book, right from the title page, there is a wholly different design scheme in place. It's like wearing a fur coat over your bathing suit. This may be a relic of a time when jackets really were just wrappers that were then flung away. The design of the book was the design of the *inside* of the book. We no longer live in that time. A book and its jacket or cover are perceived as a single entity by the reader and should be treated that way by publishers.

The Half Title

Page i is a recto (right-hand page) called the half-title page. It is defined more by what it *doesn't* include (author name, subtitle, publisher's imprint) than what it does: the title. That's all: the main title. So, what's up with this page and its redundant-yet-incomplete information? It was originally included as a sort of body double for the title page—protecting the *actually* important page that follows it. Publishers will sometimes strip a book block from its binding—to repackage unsold hardcovers as paperbacks, for instance—and that first page may be sacrificed in the process. If the full-title page is ripped out, the book is considered useless, having lost its identity and publisher's imprint (and usually the copyright page that appears on its reverse). The half title, on the other hand, is expendable.

I've always enjoyed the flexibility and minimalism of the half-title page; it's a welcome mat in front of the front door, there to greet you but not caught up in its own importance. Designers sometimes skip the title here and place an illustration, ornament, or visual element on the half-title page instead. (Some publishers don't allow this.) If really pressed to fit into a page count, a publisher might forgo the half-title page altogether, using that first recto page as the full-title page.

The Title Page

The title page officially appears on page iii, the recto (right-hand page) of the first full spread of a book. I usually think of the title page as a spread, not a single page and, if appropriate, will use the facing page for design as well. In illustrated books, the title-page spread is almost always visually interesting, an integrated part and a teaser of the design of the book. An illustration on page ii is formally called the frontispiece, but I've never heard anyone refer to it as such in all of my years as a book designer. Page ii can also be used to list the names of other books in a series or the author's previous titles.

The title page will include the title in full, the subtitle in full, and the name of the author and other important contributors to the book. The names of the editor (for a series), translator, illustrator, photographer, or other contributors often don't make it onto the front cover, and here's where you'll often find them. The title page also, importantly, includes the publisher's name and logo, which is called the publisher's imprint.

The Copyright Page

The copyright page has traditionally existed on the verso (backside) of the title page. In contemporary publishing, and primarily for illustrated or children's books, the copyright page can appear on the last page of the book instead, keeping those columns of tiny type and the never-ending information from the Library of Congress from sullying a design-focused front matter. (In ebooks, the copyright page is also often shunted to the end.) That said, readers expect the copyright page in the front matter, and if the book is a typical text-driven book, it's best kept there. The copyright page includes information about the publisher, dates of publication, copyright information and publishing history, printing information, ISBNs, the Library of Congress cataloging data, and some amount of legal jargon. It should also include art and design credits, although credit for the cover or jacket designer is usually found on the back cover or back flap. Permissions, acknowledgments, or even a dedication might land here as well if they don't fit elsewhere. The text on the copyright page is traditionally set at a size a point or two (or three) smaller than the body text. Some designers choose to take a creative approach to the copyright page. I prefer to set the type as cleanly and clearly as possible and move on.

The Dedication and Epigraph

The dedication or epigraph sits across from the copyright page. If there's both a dedication *and* an epigraph, and ample pages, I'll put the dedication across from the copyright page and the epigraph on the recto of the following spread. These short blocks of personal, often poignant, text are usually set by themselves on an otherwise empty page, and I always treat them with the greatest respect and care. Centering multiple lines of text requires careful attention, and I work to create a pleasing shape. Too-short lines at the end of a centered passage look abrupt and amateurish and are harder to scan.

The Table of Contents

The table of contents (TOC) is my favorite element in all of book design. It arrives early in the book and is a crucial orientation to what the book contains and how it is structured. Depending on how a book is organized, and how much information the author and editor choose to put up front, a TOC might be short and simple or pages long and highly detailed. The contents pages of a scholarly book on the Punic Wars, with many parts, chapters, and subheads, will look pretty different from those of a novel, which may be organized only in chapters (and may eschew a TOC entirely).

Whether simple or complex, the TOC must be a crystal-clear snapshot of the book's organization, an essential tool of navigation. A designer uses type (different fonts, sizes, a range of boldness, punctuation marks and other symbols) and page layout (columns, indentation, dividing lines, shades of gray or blocks of color) to create an outline that is easy for the reader to follow and absorb. The TOC is also an opportunity to push forward the visual character of the book.

Whether it's understated, in your face, or somewhere in between, the design here lets the reader know what to expect both literally and tonally. The TOC can not only feel like part of the book but also help create what that feel is.

A last note about the TOC: this page should be headed by the word "Contents," not "Table of Contents," which would be like saying "This is a picture of a horse" under a picture of a horse.

List of Illustrations

Some books include a listing of their illustrations and relevant information about them, and this can appear in the front matter, directly after the table of contents, or as part of the back matter.

The Dramatis Personae, Family Tree, or Map

Some books, and I love these kinds of books, preface the story with a map, family tree, or cast of characters. Coming upon one of these elements can prime the reader for what's ahead. An extended family tree or long list of characters lets the reader know that the story will be a complex, often intergenerational, saga. A map expresses that geography, boundaries, setting, or travel is an important aspect of the work. The ability to easily flip back and forth from the text to these orienting catalogs is a great example of the simple, useful technology of the bound book.

The Foreword and Preface

There are a variety of pieces of writing that may appear early in the book to frame or introduce it. The foreword is by someone other than the author and comes before the preface when both are present. The preface is the author's own piece of writing that sets the stage for the book, discussing the writing or research process but usually not engaging with the actual subject matter. An author's introduction is rightly a part of the body of the book—not the front matter—and should begin on a recto as page 1. Not all books include all these elements, and many include none of them. Preface and foreword usually use headers that are less prominent than the chapter heads that follow to help distinguish them from the primary text. As the introduction usually belongs to the main body of the book, its heading should be treated like any other chapter.

The Second Half-Title Page or Part Opener

Remember the half-title page, the redundant-yet-incomplete page that appears before the actual title page? It gets an encore! The second half-title page is the second appearance of the half-title page, this time at the end of the front matter. It's placed as a signal to the reader that the front matter is over and the main part of the book is beginning. In books with multiple sections or parts, the part opener might stand in for the second half-title page. In some books both the second half-title page *and* a part opener will appear. And if the front matter is brief—with no introductory texts or TOC—or the page count is tight, the designer might skip this page altogether.

Back Matter

The back matter (or end matter) is less sexy and more varied than the front matter; it's the back stoop, not the front porch. It usually begins with some sort of visual break that tells the reader that the main part of the book has ended, but this break is often less dramatic than earlier dividing architecture. The back matter may include appendixes, resources, a glossary, endnotes, a bibliography, a list of contributors, illustration (and other) credits, an index, and a paragraph about the type. (Huge respect to the publishers who continue to include "About the Type" information at the back of their books. How can we expect readers to appreciate design and typography if we don't tell them anything about it? I urge other serious publishers to follow suit.) At very least this is the place for acknowledgments (not in the front matter, please) and author bio, when one is included in the text ("About the Author"). Some publishers have begun acknowledging the team effort required to put out a book by including a credits page in the back matter (à la the credit roll at the end of a movie) that includes copyeditors, proofreaders, indexers, publicity and marketing folks, art and production directors, the name of the publisher, as well as those working in sales, warehousing and distribution, and administration.[1] (This is long overdue. Spread the word.) Sequencing in the back matter is less rigid than in the front—different publishing houses have different conventions for what belongs back here and in what order—although the index tends to come after most of the other elements so the reader can locate it easily.

Back matter can be information-heavy. Type is often smaller and tighter than in the primary text. In heavily referenced books, notes and bibliography can take up an enormous amount of room, and the designer, and publisher, try to make it as space-saving as possible. Most readers will not be reading straight through the back matter. Even if they do want to read every last endnote, they understand that this is secondary information and doesn't require the same easy legibility the primary text does.

The index is a hard-working part of the book, and there are pretty detailed conventions delineated in *The Chicago Manual of Style* for how to set it for maximum clarity and efficiency. Indexes should be modestly handsome and related to the typography elsewhere in a book. Beyond that, they shouldn't be overly decorated or cute if they're going to do their job properly. When planning and estimating page count for a book, designers reserve space for the index, which cannot be completed until the book is entirely set, including corrections. Saving about 5 percent of the entire page count is safe, but it's not a precise calculation. I sometimes find myself with a shorter index and a lot of pages to fill, in which case I set it with large type (never larger than the body text though) and spaced airily to fill the room. If the index turns out to be longer than expected—the more common scenario—I may need to go quite small with type size and tight with line spacing.

All books end on a verso facing either the endpapers (for a hardcover book) or the inside of the back cover (in a paperback). A blank last page is common or, if the book is tight on space, it might scoop up the last bit of the back matter. Some publishers might include a marketing page back here. In illustrated and design-forward books, the designer might leave the reader with a final, visual nod—illustration, ornament, photograph—that brings closure.

The Body of the Book

Between the front matter and the back matter is the body of the book, the real meat, the raison d'être. The intention and function of a book determines a lot about the way it unfolds. A novel works one way and a travel guide another. Books with images are designed differently than those without. Books meant to be dipped in and out of have different needs than those meant to be read straight through. An author's choices around structure are as fundamental to their ideas as their choices around language.

Designers get to, and must, bring a visual, organizational, *and* editorial eye to their work. While I haven't understood the content of every book I've ever designed—I admit, the one on chakras was beyond me—I work hard to understand how the author has chosen to organize and communicate their thoughts. Design should always respond to the editorial impulse and not take the text somewhere it doesn't want to go. As designers try to impose a visual organization on a text, its underlying logic is revealed. Occasionally a book survives all the rounds of editing and copyediting and still has leaks in its hull—that is, the organization is confusing or not quite sound. It's in the design phase that this will become unavoidably clear and, hopefully, remedied.

Parts

In many books, chapters are the largest unit of division. But in others there is a level above that, the part, which might be designated "Part 1" or "The Early Years" or perhaps "The Recipes." If there is a part 1 there will be a part 2 (and maybe parts 3, 4, and 5) later in the book. "The Early Years" will probably be followed by "The Middle Years" and so on. On the other hand, "The Recipes" might be the only part that appears.

In the hierarchy of the book, parts are the highest level and must make their dominance apparent. The pages their titles are placed on are called part openers. While a chapter usually begins on a fresh page, a part opener will occupy two or three pages—an entire spread for the part opener itself, followed by a left-hand page that is left blank, with the chapter beginning on the next right-hand page. All the empty space around the part opener sends a message: I'm important! A part opener might consist of only a title; it might consist of only *Part 1*. Picture all that paper with so few words on it. It's like the expanse of land around an estate while the rest of the village is living on top of each other.

Not all part openers feature just a few words. Some have a paragraph, or a few paragraphs, of accompanying text, in which case the use of negative space might not create as strong a signal. Part titles are often set in type that is bigger, bolder, or in a different font than chapter headings. Any accompanying text should also be differentiated. To continue with my medieval village analogy: The nobles don't wear the same clothes as the villagers. It's their fine silks and leathers that communicates their status.

Chapters

Chapters are the most familiar division of a book, an important organizer and welcome pause for both writers and their readers. In most books, a new chapter begins on a new page (and when it doesn't, and a new chapter starts up again on the same page as the old one, it's hard not to feel robbed). Whether chapters begin on the next *available* page or only appear on the dominant, right-hand pages of a spread is usually a matter of house style or author preference. In either case, the chapter title will begin some ways down the page, the empty space signaling that something notable is happening. A book may have six long chapters or sixty short ones, and the treatment of the chapter opener will reflect this rhythm—longer chapters demand a more emphatic break, a rest stop after a long climb.

The chapter display is all the pieces that make up the chapter heading. This might be as simple as a number. Or a number plus a

CHAPTER 1

Breakfast

THE MOST IMPORTANT MEAL OF THE DAY

"If there is one thing I am fond of for breakfast,
it is a soft-boiled egg," said Father.

RUSSELL HOBAN, *BREAD AND JAM FOR FRANCES*

Complex chapter displays can begin to resemble a seven-layer cake.

title. Or a number, title, subtitle, range of dates, quote, attribution of a quote, and the weather at the scene. Chapter displays can be maximalist or minimalist; some authors eliminate all titling for their chapters.

To my eyes, when chapter displays are centered, they command the space and are full of their own importance, like stretching your arms along the back of the chairs on either side of you. When they're sent flush left they're more understated, sharing alignment with the rest of the text. I can spend a long time fiddling with the details. Should the chapter number be styled as "Chapter One," "One," or simply "1"? Add brackets around that number? Period or no period? (Designers typically have leeway on such display issues, regardless of what the manuscript says.) And how should the chapter title relate to the number above and the text below? The more information there is to manage, the more convoluted the relationships and type styling become.

Chapter titles are like miniature book titles and, as with cover design, the language used—the number of words and the actual words—will push the design in one way or another. Short businesslike titles like "Type," "Covers," or "Inside the Book" feel (and will be styled differently) than chapter titles like "A Short History of Typographical Variations" and "Page Elements and Make-Up of Pages."[2] Short or long or somewhere in between, consistency in the structure and length of (part and) chapter titles is good editorial form and will come with the added benefit of a more cohesive design.

One more characteristic of chapter openers: the first paragraph of body text after the chapter display is typically not indented. Designers often give this text additional emphasis, a way of saying: "Start reading here!" This can take the form of a drop cap or raised cap or bolded (or otherwise contrasting) first few words or first full line. The busier the chapter display (and the text itself), the simpler this introduction need be.

Subheads

Many nonfiction books, including this one, rely on a series of divisions and subdivisions inside the chapter to express kinship and distinction between different kinds of information. Chopping up text into sections and giving those sections names organizes information, creates a quick outline for the reader, and makes it easier to hop around to areas of interest. The titles of these sections are called subheads (or subheadings or headers or just heads). A book may need one set of headers or it may need a few. Before diving in, designers determine the number and complexity of headings that are used throughout a book and work out a formula for every level. In a complex book, like a field guide, this can run to six or more levels and requires a lot of fancy footwork. How headings relate to one another—this is more important than that but less important than this—can be a complicated formula to concoct and communicate and, when done well, is one of the most valuable skills that designers bring to a text.

Within a manuscript, subheads are named for their level within the hierarchy: H1 for the highest level, H2 for the next, H3 for the next, and so on (they can also be labeled A-head, B-head, C-head, etc.). Of course these tags don't end up on the printed page, and designers must make their status clear to readers in some way. The more important a

H2 or B-head

The Big Cheese

Called an H1 or A-head, the top-level heading is usually the largest and/or boldest of the headings. It gets the most space around it and sometimes is center aligned, differentiating it from the text below.

IMPORTANT DIVISION

The H2 (or B-head) signals a secondary subdivision of the text. Here, the heading shows its status with a bold sans serif set in all caps. It has space above and below it but has been shifted over to a left alignment.

Further Subdivision
Here, the H3 (or C-head) shares the same font and size as the body text. Its placement on its own line and its boldness create some authority.

Even more hierarchy. This fourth-level heading (H4 or D-head) is showing its subservience by sharing the line with its related text (designers call this a run-in heading). It is distinguished from the type that follows by italics and a medium boldness.

> There are infinite ways—typographic and spatial—to express or reveal the hierarchy of a text. Each should suit its subject and the voice of the author.

heading, the more visible or obvious it should be and the more distinct from the text around it. Most writers and editors use some form of visual hierarchy while they're writing: you might put your most important headings in all caps, the next level in bold, and the level below that in italic. You understand that the way headings look communicates their rank and that this is integral to meaning.

But there's more to life than just bold and italic. Alongside visual structure, designers create visual style. Type communicates explicitly ("this heading is more important than that heading") and implicitly ("this content is lighthearted" or "this content is deadly serious"). Extra bold has a different feel than light, and all lowercase says something different from all uppercase. How space is meted out, both above and below headings, creates meaningful attachments and distinctions. Books with many levels of hierarchy are more complex to design because there are so many more typographic choices to make and stylings to invent.

My take on subheads: they should be relatively short. The space that is created by a short line is part of what makes it identifiable *as* a heading. Short heads also allow readers to quickly grasp what they're about to read. Headings that take a full line length or—ugh—more than a single line will be less effective and should usually be reworked.

Paragraphs

Below the chapter titles and headings is a whole lot of text. Designers usually refer to this primary text as the body text or running text. In most books (Samuel Beckett excepted) this text is broken into paragraphs for the benefit of both reader and writer. As authors and editors know, the places where paragraphs break is intuitive and expressive. Books with long paragraphs feel different from ones with short—there is more space, both visual and metaphysical. Designers can signal these breaks through a variety of methods. The most common, by far, is a hard return to end a paragraph followed by an indentation at the start of the new one. How much to indent is a judgment call: enough, not too much. The longer the line, the more indent is needed to make an impression.

Indenting paragraphs is such a familiar convention that you might not realize that there are other options. For instance, designers (or writers) can eschew indentation and, instead, add a line space between paragraphs. This is common practice in letters and emails

Designers decide how deep to make the paragraph indent.

and other short texts, and it emphasizes the independence of chunks of text. Some novels use this graphic device deliberately to reinforce a narrative concept. In most instances, authors want running text to feel connected, not independent, and indentation is a better choice. It's also more economical in terms of space. All those empty lines add up to a lot of extra paper when you're talking about an 80,000-word manuscript. What's never an option is doing both. An extra line space is a signal and an indentation is a signal and used together, that's one too many signals.

Throughout the history of books, other methods have been tried. A designer could skip indentation as well as the hard return and choose instead to add a pilcrow (¶) to indicate the end/beginning of a new paragraph. This keeps the flow between paragraphs (and thoughts) exceedingly congruent, creating a text monolith, which may feel uninviting or intimidating to a reader. I'd love to see the look on the face of an author who gets their first layout back with only pilcrows between the paragraphs. Other ways to begin a paragraph might be outdenting—having the first line extend out from the text block, rather than in—or beginning each paragraph with a drop cap, ornament, or bolded letter or word. Because the hard return/indentation convention is so expected in modern books, any choice but that one will call attention to itself.

Breaks in the Text

Many writers want to indicate a change of idea or shift in the narrative that is stronger than that of a new paragraph but not as strong as a chapter break. This is called an editorial or section break. Section breaks can be indicated by simply skipping a line (or two or four), then starting the text up again, usually with an unindented paragraph. The more space between the sections, the more independent from one another they will be perceived to be. Sometimes designers will make the first few words of this new paragraph bold or in small caps to underscore the idea: *new thought*.

Some designers, by request of the author or not, will add an ornament between sections to emphasize the break more forcefully. Common choices for an ornament might be three asterisks or bullets (this is called, delightfully, a dinkus), a thin line, a fleur-de-lis, or a dingbat. Some authors (or designers) will use a small thematic drawing or piece of line art as a section break. This can be charming in certain situations, cloying in others.

Extracts/Block Text

Material quoted for more than a sentence or two is usually set off in block text to distinguish other voices from the author's. Block text is individuated from running text by a line space above and below and is indented on both the right and left sides, or just on the left if the trim size is small. This is plenty to signal that block text is just a little distinct from other text. Mostly you want the reader to flow in and right back out. In some books there may be reason to emphasize these extracts a little more, in which case I might set them italics or in a semibold face, or one point smaller than the body text.

Lists and Tables

Lists and tables are a mainstay of certain kinds of nonfiction books, very common in business and self-help and in all kinds of books that include instructions. They're a piece of architecture on the page and look different (and read differently) than running text. Writers might toss them in—lists are easier to write than prose—but designers must labor over them.

There are three kinds of lists: bulleted (or unordered), numbered (or ordered), and keyword (or definition; lists that begin with a key word or phrase). Designers keep lists clear and skimmable by styling them simply, particularly the bullets. Numbers and bullets should be small and understated, never cute or scene-stealing (check marks are a no-no). The idea is to draw attention to the approaching bear, not the hand that's pointing at it. Authors, ask yourself: Do you really need to number that list? If a list isn't literally sequential, or a top-ten kind of thing, simple bullets are a cleaner read. Keyword lists, when appropriate, are efficient because the keywords (or phrases) do the job of the bullet or number, drawing the eye down the list, while also providing content. Lists with emphasized keywords don't also need bullets.

Lists organize data vertically; tables, in two dimensions. When you create a default table in Microsoft Word, the result looks like a jail cell, with bars keeping each bite of information locked in its own pen. The thing with tables is that the architecture is there to hold up the building—we're not admiring the Taj Mahal here. Heavy lines, over-emphasized stripes, and other bling can steal the show, when it's the data we want to shine. The information designer Edward Tufte calls these decorations "chartjunk": "Promoters imagine that numbers and

Designing Lists

BULLETED LISTS

- Bullets should be small and understated, never cute.
- Items should "hang" off the bullet and can be indented on the right (but needn't be).
- If items are short, they don't need additional space between them.
- Lists should be set left aligned, not justified (see page 126)

NUMBERED LISTS

1. Only number lists if the numbers add meaning.

2. If numbers are differentiated from the text, they should not be overly prominent. They are essentially bullets.

3. Numbers can be followed by a period, a closing parenthesis, a slash, or a dash, but they don't need any of those things.

KEYWORD LISTS

Punctuation. I often choose a period—or no punctuation at all—rather than a colon after keywords. Why use two dots when one, or none, does the job?

Emphasis. Keywords should be set in bold, italic, or a contrasting font so they stand out.

Spacing. Definition lists don't "hang." They can be indented from the left, but they don't need to be. Space between items is usually necessary.

details are boring, dull, and tedious, requiring ornament to enliven. . . . If the numbers are boring, then you've got the wrong numbers."[3]

Table design should guide the reader along its throughways, emphasizing the relationships between and within data. Lines between columns but not between rows will create one kind of emphasis. Reverse it, and another set of relationships is stressed. Alternating colors (or shades of gray) of columns or rows (zebra striping) can make it easy to follow along without additional lines. As always, negative space telegraphs status and draws the eye. Headers can be given more room than the body cells, but everything in a table should have a decent buffer. Tight cells will make everyone feel itchy.

Sidebar

Planning Ahead for Sidebars

Many aspects of book design bridge editorial and design concerns. What text should go in sidebars and where the sidebars belong are decisions made by the author and editor, sometimes without much thought about how those choices will end up on the page. I have worked on books that designate more sidebars than primary text on some spreads, a confusing situation for a reader and a nearly impossible one for a designer. Editors who are conscious of page design, or who huddle with designers or art directors when thinking through books with many elements, will structure text in the editing phase in ways that result in sensible and elegant design solutions.

Sidebars and Other Asides

Some nonfiction books have content that exists alongside, but independent of, the primary running text. A book about the Renaissance might step aside for half a page to relate a biography of Michelangelo. A business book might interrupt the body text to present a list of goals or questions. This kind of independent text is usually called a sidebar, whether it hangs out alongside the primary text or not. It can run from a few lines to half a page or more. Full-page sidebars are often referred to as features or, simply, essays. Another variety of aside is the pull quote, a short phrase or sentence pulled out of the text and given its own space. A pull quote that is too long basically becomes a sidebar.

Reference and other illustrated books often use sidebars, and their oversized pages provide plenty of room for secondary columns alongside running text. In a standard 6 × 9–inch book, though, there's no room for a second column and these passages will usually sit in the same block as the rest of the text. In some cases, an aside might stick halfway in, halfway out of a text column, requiring text to wrap around it (wrapped text requires a lot of finessing). In all cases, the designer must make clear: "Hey! *This* text is different from *that* text."

Font choice and styling is how designers differentiate text for the reader. How do you know that the tip at the end of the recipe is a little extra note and not part of the method? It looks different. That may mean it's set in a different font or it may mean the same font is being styled in a distinctive way—set in italic, bolder, larger, in all caps. Design choices are made within the language that the book has established. A kid's cookbook and a book on changing careers may both include tips treated as sidebars. Clearly, they will need to be handled differently.

An outlined box is the classic idea of how to indicate a sidebar, but not necessarily the best one—this approach says "high school textbook" to me. A trade book, even a serious one, can have a little more subtlety or style. A line above and below is more dignified than a box. A line just above the set-off text can sometimes work. A shaded box behind type (no lines) is calm and pleasing, although in a one-color book it can be tricky to dial in the right shade. Make the box too dark and the text will be hard to read. Make it too light and it will not be visible enough. An invisible box—a big cushion of space around the type—can work if there's enough room. If I have color at my disposal, I'm golden.

Hey! *This* text is different from *that* text.

Footnotes

As a reader, I get why footnotes are superior to endnotes—who wants to keep flipping to the back of the book to find information?—but the visual havoc they can wreak on the page is maddening. The ideal footnote is available for those who are interested but not a distraction for those who aren't. Striking this balance is challenging. Fitting really long (or multiple) footnotes all on the same page as their reference is sometimes impossible. Splitting footnotes onto more than a single page can result in two narrative streams, where the footnote text is pages ahead of the body text. Adding the typographic fussiness of asterisks and daggers and tiny type makes the page more chaotic.* Many authors use footnotes to provide important context, sources, and secondary information, but let's score one for ebooks—their hyperlinked and pop-up footnotes are clearly superior to the limitations of the printed page.

*Some better designers than me place footnotes in the outside margins rather than at the foot of the page (shoulder notes?). This has the benefit of setting footnotes adjacent to the relevant text and relieving the page of all the fuss of the standard system. But two big caveats: books designed to have footnotes in the shoulder need to have generous outside margins. The page size and the width of the text column must oblige this only occasional feature. Even with a wide outer margin, these footnotes will need to be relatively brief. If long footnotes are in the cards, this is not going to be an elegant solution.

The Page

There's nothing like seeing your text transformed from a Word document to a designed book page. There's so much authority rooted in that iconic layout: running head, text block, page number. It's unmistakable and powerful. But it also may be so familiar that it's practically invisible. While you can recognize a book page and you've certainly read one, perhaps you've never actually *looked* at one. It doesn't need to become a habit—(most) books are made for reading, not looking—but just this once, pull out a book, open it up, and notice what's happening.

Margins and the Text Block

The structure of a book page is like a picture inside a frame. The margins surround the text on all sides (that's the frame), containing and presenting it: the action's in here. Margins, like other frames, are buffers, separating the text, visually, from the world. Bigger margins offer

Outer margin

more protection. Practically, the size of the margins is a negotiation between beauty and efficiency. The more breathing room around the text, the prettier it looks and the more pleasant it is to read. The tighter the margins, the more words will fit on the page. More words on the page equals fewer pages overall. Fewer pages means a cheaper book to produce. Mass-market paperbacks are recognizable for their small type and tight margins. As in a Victorian drawing room, a big frame usually announces status.

The printing—usually text, sometimes images—is set in columns. Pages can have multiple columns, but in your standard 6 × 9–inch text-driven book, there is a single one. The text block sits fairly centrally but not usually exactly centered. Objects placed in the vertical center of a page appear too low, so the bottom margin should be larger than the top one, acting like a bolster at the foot of the page. The outside margins are a place for your thumbs (and your notes) and should be wide enough to hold them without covering any letters. The inner margins, called the gutter, keep words from sliding into the crease of the binding. But if the gutter is *too* wide, the text blocks start to feel

The Anatomy of a Page

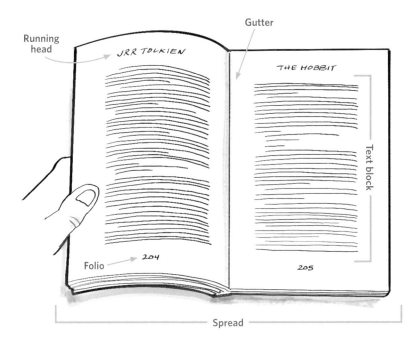

disconnected. The spread is a unit and the energy should pull text blocks toward each other, not apart.

Running Heads and Feet

Running heads (or running feet) are the short titles that appear on nearly every page. These signposts identify the name of the chapter, part, or title of the book on which they appear and help the reader stay oriented. In nonfiction books, particularly complex ones with chapters inside parts, they're important navigational tools. They're called heads when they're set at the top of the text block and feet when below it. What's included in the heads (or feet) is often designated by the book's editor or a publisher's house style. It can be the book title on the left-hand page and the chapter title on the right-hand page. Or a part title on the left-hand page and a chapter title on the right-hand page. Or some other combination of a book's divisions and identifiers. Running heads don't appear on a book's initial pages (a title page with a running head would be redundant indeed; a table of contents with a running head is a complete faux pas), and the pieces of front and back matter that do sport running titles often depart from the system in the body of the book (both right- and left-hand pages of the bibliography, for instance, might have the running head "bibliography" regardless of the convention in the rest of the book). In fiction, running heads usually display the author's name on the left-hand page and the title of the book on the right or are dropped altogether.

Authors and editors rarely comment on the look of running heads (or feet), but they're elements that I spend a lot of time on. How they look and where they're placed impacts the balance and sensibility of the page. A centered running head is classic. Aligning it, instead, with the outside margin can feel more casual, modern, or minimal. A running head crowns the page while a running foot will anchor it. Caps (or small caps) versus title case, italics versus roman, a contrasting typeface or the same one as the primary text are all possibilities. The running head (along with the page number) will occasionally sit in the outside margin, particularly in books with a wider trim size and, when placed there, is called a running shoulder. Of course.

Page Numbers

Almost every book, whether or not it includes running heads or feet, will include page numbers (the exception being short children's picture books). The page number, sometimes referred to as the folio, is an essential part of the technology of the book, allowing readers to reference, cross-reference, keep track of, and search out relevant information. Numbers should be obvious on the page, but not intrusive, and easy to see when flipping through. It is typical for the page number to be aligned with the outside edge of the text block, either above or below, which is the easiest place to find them. Centering page numbers below the text block is also common.

The page number is foremost functional but, like the running head, frames and decorates the text block and the page itself. When

Folio

designing a page, I think about how this small element should look, where it should sit, and how that affects the balance of the page and spread. On a text page with so few elements, the styling and placement of the page number is a major event.

Needless to say, page numbers should not move around from page to page—their number-one purpose is to be easily located. But there is one exception. In books where the page number appears in the top margin, it drops into the bottom margin on chapter openers (called a drop folio). Chapter titles are their own signposts and so don't require, and should never include, running heads or feet. Some designers dispense with the drop folio as well.

Setting Type

For the first four hundred years of printed books, type was set by building up the text, letter by metal letter and line by physical line. Compositors (or typesetters), as the people who set type are called (still), considered how big the type, how long the line, how much space between words and between lines *physically*. Bigger type meant bigger pieces of metal. Longer lines meant a physically longer block of type to create and move, print, and re-sort.

Digital typesetting, which is how all commercial books today are composited, retains this attention to detail. Contemporary book design is cqually interested in the size of type and length of line because these are the difference between an easily readable page and one where the reader is stumbling, distracted, or repelled. "It is the way we read that is the yardstick for book design, not the traditions, ideologies or opinions of typographers,"[4] says one expert. Aside from simple clarity, the intended readers' age range, use, expectations, and level of vision will determine many typesetting choices. (Ebooks allow for more flexibility than print when it comes to accessibility options. I'll discuss that more in chapter 6.) Note that the discussion that follows is geared toward the English language, which is what I know about. Other languages certainly have other, distinct, typesetting needs.

What follows are the things designers think about when setting running text on a page. These are the seemingly small and mostly unrecognized acts of artistry that allow the type to fade away so the story can emerge.

Line Length

Designers, like poets, pay a lot of attention to their lines. When setting up a page of text, we consider what would be a comfortable reading line for *this* text on *this*-sized page in *this* font at *this* size. Bigger type can take, and may need, a longer line; smaller type will require a shorter one. The length of a line (called its measure) is related to its tempo and functionality. Compare the length of a line in a typical novel to one in a typical newspaper. Newspapers are meant to be read, or skimmed, quickly. Sentences are short. Ideas are factual. Books are meant to be immersive. The ideas may be complex and take longer to unwind. Even the words used may be longer. A longer line length slows the reader down and lets them take a long hot bath in the narrative.[5]

For narrative books, the rule of thumb is that a line can hold forty-five to seventy-five characters for a comfortable read, and the ideal line is, supposedly, sixty-six characters.[6] (This is fine to know, but I don't count my characters; I make the judgment call with my eyes.) The text in books that are meant to be skimmed is often broken into multiple columns with shorter lines. As any high schooler will tell you, it's hard to skim the longer lines of a novel. A dictionary is a classic example of a multiple-column layout, and this is common in large-format, reference, or instructional books across categories.

In books with big pages, overly long lines are sometimes a problem. I've had authors ask me to extend the line length so they can fit more words on a page (for instance, this might be a request for recipe headnotes in cookbooks, where authors always want more space and designers are often trying to keep it from them with arguments about line lengths). The thing is, lines of text that go on too long are like people who go on too long: exhausting. I know I'm doing my authors a favor by keeping line length appropriate, easy to read, and welcoming.

Line Spacing

Leading is the traditional term for the amount of space between lines of text. When it's too tight, it's hard to read. When it's too loose, it's hard to read. Finding the sweet spot is part of the designer's job.

Leading is the traditional term for the amount of space between lines of text. When it's too tight, it's hard to read. When it's too loose, it's hard to read. Finding the sweet spot is part of the designer's job.

Leading is the traditional term for the amount of space

between lines of text. When it's too tight, it's hard to read.

When it's too loose, it's hard to read. Finding the sweet

spot is part of the designer's job.

Line Spacing

Another way to make lines of type readable is to attend to the amount of space between them. This is properly called the lead (pronounced *led*), and adjusting it is leading (rhymes with *sledding*). The word comes from the nonprinting pieces of lead that were placed between lines of type when books were set by hand. More lead, more white space between the lines. Lines of type need a little distance; it would be very annoying if, as you read, the tops of the *d*'s crashed into the stems of the *p*'s in the line above. Beyond this obvious blooper, when lines are too tightly packed, they become like a fortress, barring entry. A reader will sometimes lose their way and drop down a line right in the middle of a paragraph. And when there is too much space between lines— even worse! Loosely spaced lines lose their relationship to one another, and the reader has to work too hard to keep track as they move from one line down to the next. Longer lines will need more leading and shorter lines need less. Bigger type will require more air around it, smaller type can be cozier. In books of straight text, lines will be uniformly leaded down the page. Books with various kinds of text on a page may employ a variety of different leading.

Alignment

Alignment refers to the shape of a text block. When text lines up cleanly on both left and right sides, making a neat rectangle, that is called fully justified (or sometimes, simply justified) text. It is how you expect most book pages to look. But there are other options for text alignment. Text can look more like a flag—straight along the left edge and rippling along the right. This is how text looks in your word processing document and it's called flush left or ragged right. The flag can also wave the other way, in which case it is called flush right. It would be unusual, and annoying, to read a long passage of text set flush right because each line begins in a different place, a lot of work for the reader. (This is the case for English and other left-to-right reading languages. For languages that read right-to-left, the opposite will be true.) Text can also be centered within the frame. Designers often use center alignment for titles, headings, and short passages like quotes or epigraphs. Centering longer passages of text can be tricky, as the lines start to form distracting UFO-like shapes. These passages can take a lot of tending to look good.

Each form of alignment has its pros and cons. Justified text is easy to read because you know where the line begins and you know where it will end. Moving down from line to line is a breeze. It also uses space efficiently, taking up the full length of the text block on every line. But justified text has its issues. To make that clean rectangular shape, a designer, or more accurately their layout program, stretches and smushes the spaces between words to create an even edge. Mostly this works, with judicious use of hyphenation, and sometimes it doesn't. You may have noticed this occasionally in your reading—big gaps in a line or sentences that barely seem to have a break between words.

Alignment

This text is fully justified. It spans the full line from left to right and ends up looking like a neat block.

Fully justified

This text is left aligned. The space between each word is consistent, but the end of each line is not.

Flush left

This text is right aligned. It is awkward to read because each line begins in a different place.

Flush right

This text is centered. It needs a lot of tending to keep both edges natural and easy to follow.

Centered

When gaps in lines run down a page, it's called a river. Rivers are distracting and to be avoided. The shorter the line length, the less spaces there are to massage and the more troublesome this issue becomes. (Talking to you, *The New Yorker*.) One of the primary jobs of the compositor, typesetter, or designer is to scan each and every page and do what we can to reduce lines that feel tighter or looser than those around them.

Flush-left text doesn't have this problem: lines end where a break makes most sense, and spaces between words remain natural throughout. But flush-left text can, when untended, form awkward shapes and abrupt cliffs along the ragged edge. Designers monitor and adjust their paragraphs to prevent these distractions. We are looking for a gentle ripple, not a torn hem.

Designers also use alignment as a way to distinguish different pieces of text from one another—a centered header stands out from the text below it, a sidebar or caption might be left aligned in contrast to justified body text. A special quote might sit centered or even right aligned, noticeably different from other text.

Line Breaks

One time an author, reading her first set of typeset pages, said to me: "Ugh, can we get rid of all those ugly hyphens at the ends of the lines?" She'd been looking at hyphens her whole life and only now, in her own book, did she *see* them. Hyphens are used within writing to create compound words, of course. Hyphens are also used typographically to divide a word at the end of a line to in order to improve the word spacing within lines of (justified) text or calm the rag (in ragged text). Most publishers have a house style for when and how often to use hyphens for line breaks or follow the guidelines in *The Chicago Manual of Style* (see page 204 for more on hyphenation rules). Rules for breaking lines—like all rules—sometimes also need to be broken.

What I explained to the newbie author is that hyphenation is a typographic necessity, allowing designers to create more natural spacing between words on a line, smoothing the way to a pleasant, readable page. Readers, habituated to hyphens, find them unremarkable and glide on by. A hyphen stack at the end of a paragraph (three or more lines in a row ending in a hyphen) is undesirable because it draws attention to the hyphens, but it's also not the end of the world. I find gappy or smushed lines much more distracting. The allergy to hyphenation found in some editorial circles is unfounded. When the rules for hyphenation are smartly set, and a proofreader reviews hyphenated words for sense, breaking words across lines is a great asset to the text and a force for good in the world.

Emphasis

Authors often want to emphasize particular words and phrases to highlight concepts within the body of the paragraph. Bold face; italics; all caps; small caps; and shifts in font, size, and color are familiar ways to do this. Italics is the classic, and least obtrusive, way to indicate a change within running text. Small caps is useful for abbreviations or acronyms or when all caps is beckoning (all caps, we know from the internet, is like shouting in the reader's ear). Bold is useful in reference books and usually distracting in narrative text, better left for headers. Underlining is a throwback to typewriter days and rarely seen in professionally typeset pages. Emphasized words should wink at the reader from the page—"hi there!"—not barrage them.

The Well-Groomed Spread

Designers want every page of the book to look its best, keeping the reader moving without stopping at moments of confusion or distraction. A neat and tidy page does not begin with a short line at the top. A useful page does not leave the title of a list at the bottom and the rest of the list on the next page. If the header "Best Things to Say to Your Boss" is left alone on the bottom of the right-hand page, it's simply too suspenseful for the reader to have to flip the page to see item one.

A "widow" is the last line of a paragraph that ends at the top of a page. An "orphan" is the first line of a paragraph abandoned at the bottom of a page.[7] Designers create a smooth page (and smooth reading experience) by keeping both these distractions to a minimum. Really short lines also mar the page. Many publishers require a certain number of characters on the last line of any paragraph (somewhere in the realm of five to ten) to prevent these "runt lines."

In books of running text, the text on facing pages should always end on the same line. This is called balancing spreads, or aligning columns. If one page of a spread is a line or two shorter than the other, the reader will perceive this as the end of a chapter or section or, at the least, a break in the text. If it is none of these things, that would be a serious miscue. Some kinds of books can break this rule—you wouldn't expect poems on facing pages to end on the same line. And when text is broken up by lots of headings and subheadings, as in this book, allowing unaligned columns is often a good choice.

When the same word appears at the beginning or end of two or more consecutive lines, this stacking can cause understandable confusion in the reader, making them skip or redouble a line. Designers scan for and try to avoid word stacks and hyphen stacks when possible.

One of the truisms of book design is that you have to work with what you've been given. We don't get to adjust the content to our needs. No matter how completely I've worked out a design, there will be some unfortunate situations. When dealing with hundreds of pages and thousands of words, scanning and solving for widows, orphans, runt lines, overly wide or tight lines, and aligned columns is one of the most time-consuming, often boring, sometimes frustrating, and necessary parts of a designer's (or compositor's) job. Keeping text columns aligned across the spread trumps all other concerns (in books of narrative text), sometimes resulting in a widow or orphan or a line that is too tight or too loose. Book design is often a matter of compromise, little deals with the devil, and I almost never complete a book without some regrettable passages that I simply cannot resolve to my liking.

Interior Decorating

Decorative elements and ornamentation have been around since books were written and illuminated by scribes. Ornamentation might include swashes, swirls, curlicues, fancy lines or frames, vines, leaves, and flowers, geometric patterns, and typographic extras like brackets, asterisks, and bullets. These sorts of elements, when used with restraint and intention, can add visual interest to a page, create spatial balance, or communicate some concept about the text (it's historical, it's playful, it's fantastical). Ornaments can be used to decorate chapter headings, title pages, section breaks, or plopped in the middle of a blank page like a cairn. A little goes a long way. Ornaments should never become the focus—William Morris excepted—that honor goes to the text. The ivy that grows along my back fence and consistently threatens to take over the entire garden is a lesson in keeping things pared down and open to the air.

One of the places I've noticed tension between designers and word people is around what it means for a book or a page to look "designed." To me, a book that expresses affinity with the sensibility of the text and is easy to read is successful. (Illustrated and design-forward books will have some different demands for design; more on that in the next chapter.) And yet it's not unusual to be asked by writers and editors for "more design." Sometimes this means: Can the display type be more distinctive or playful, can contrast and emphasis be more dramatic, and, most commonly, can we add some nonessential ornamentation? I suspect that nondesigners, not quite getting the *actual* work of book design, see the inclusion of ornament as proof of design—it is "extra," the designer must have thought to put it there, therefore the designer is thinking! If this book gives you nothing else, I hope it helps you understand that, ornamentation or not, the designer *is* thinking about a thousand things. A clean page isn't evidence of lack of thought or skill—often quite the opposite.

Chapter 5

Illustrated Books

Illustrated books are books with images. But in publishing circles the term implies more than that, suggesting a book that has been produced with greater attention to its materials, production, and design. A cheap paperback can have a tacky charm; the words still resonate. But for illustrated books to succeed, they must be objects worth having. They're books that might be returned to again and again (like a cookbook) or prized as an aesthetic object and set beside the crystal vase on the coffee table. An important part of their value is in the printing and binding, the feel of the paper, the reproduction of color, and the beauty or inherent interest of the images. Design is the glue that holds it all together.

Designing illustrated books is a complicated project requiring more time, more people, and more planning than your straightforward text-only book. The most satisfying illustrated books come to be because editorial, artistic, and design ideas are developed alongside each other. They don't get beautiful by accident.

Illustrated How?

Illustrated book is an umbrella term that covers a lot of ground. Art books, children's picture books, graphic novels, and some "lifestyle" books are art-driven (the art is the focus), while textbooks, popular reference, field guides, and how-to books may be art-accompanied (the images playing more of a supporting role). Lots of pictures, few words is a different energy than few pictures, lots of words or, as is often the case, lots of pictures and lots of words.

What kinds of images, how many, and where they'll come from or who will make them are basic editorial and design questions for illustrated books. Is that cookbook going to include twenty-five photographs or seventy-five? Is that book on knitting going to include watercolors or line art? Is that children's book going to be illustrated by Mo Willems or Chris Van Allsburg? (If only.) The answers will speak to function, audience, and intention. Books where images are the side dish will be approached differently than those where art is the main course. Some images are informative, providing content that the words don't or can't. Other images are decorative, establishing mood more than supplying information. Some art is Art.

Some illustrated books begin with a set of preexisting images—an artist's work, a person's or institution's archive, or the mushroom photos you've taken on a decade's worth of hikes. In other books the text exists first and images must be found or created. Children's picture books are often bought as a manuscript only (most publishers prefer to choose the illustrator for kids' books). Cookbooks, also, often begin with no images and only the barest amount of text. Editor, art director, and author will work together to settle on a visual style and choose a photographer. For cookbook photography, this also means finding a studio with a kitchen; finalizing recipe lists (and the recipes themselves); sourcing ingredients; cooking the food; making it look gorgeous; finding appropriate plates, glasses, silverware, serving bowls, linens, and surfaces; setting a table (or many different tables); and, only then, shooting the images. You can't believe how much effort goes into the production of a cookbook. For all books where images don't already exist, an image maker will need to be identified, agreed upon, art-directed, managed, and paid.

When starting work on an illustrated book, there are all sorts of questions that the designer, and everyone on the team, must answer. The choices have consequences for budgets, timelines, contributors, page counts, and design (see the sidebar on page 136).

Vision and Planning

Illustrated books require a great deal of organization and a team effort from the beginning. In the best situations, authors, editors, art directors, and designers huddle early on to discuss ideas—this is the fun part! "Let's imagine what this book could be!" Do the images already

Working with Images

When starting out on a book that will include images, the team should discuss the following questions.

What is the *role* of the images?

☐ Focus of or reason for the book   ☐ Equal to text   ☐ Decoration

What is the *function* of the images?

☐ Information   ☐ Art   ☐ Decoration

Do the images already exist?

NO	YES
☐ Where will they come from?	☐ Do we have permission to use them?
☐ Who will make them?	☐ Is it a single artist or multiple artists?
☐ Is stock imagery an option?	☐ What style(s) are they?
☐ What style should they be?	☐ What medium(s) are they?
☐ What medium should they be?	☐ Are they high-resolution?
☐ What's the budget?	☐ Do they need to be digitized?

How many images?

Do they need Photoshop (or other technical) work?

How large should/must they appear?

Can they be cropped?

How will the book be printed?   ☐ 1 color   ☐ 2 color   ☐ 4 color

---

exist or will they need to be created? Will the author create (or provide) them, or will another person bring their creativity to the project? (And who will that be?) How many images makes sense? How many can we afford? How much text is there (or will there be)? How long is this book going to be? Conceiving and planning illustrated books is an editorial *and* a design proposition. It's also a question of production. Printing and binding options may be a larger piece of the vision and the budget than for other types of books and must be worked out at an early stage.

What Size?

Illustrated books vary in size more than text-driven books. Art books are often on the larger side so images can be seen in all their glory. In books where there are lots of images and text, a bigger page will also offer the most real estate. But there's a balance to be struck between roomy and unwieldy. Some art books, in their attempt to be lavish, end up hulking. And function should always steer size considerations. If the book is meant to be used while hiking, it will need to be small enough to fit easily into a backpack or even hip pocket.

Different profiles bring with them different feels, but if images already exist, their needs and proportion will dictate, at least in part, the proportion and trim size of the book. If the art is all portrait orientation, or all landscape, the book's proportion will be chosen for a nice fit. But it's not unusual for art to arrive in all different sizes and proportions. Designers can help figure out a page size that makes the most sense. If art doesn't exist already, the team can choose a trim size and have images made to measure.

Mood Boards

And if the art doesn't already exist, how do you figure out what it should be? Sometimes authors come with specific ideas or artists they want to work with (sometimes the authors *are* the artists). Often, though, they don't, and it's usually the design team, together with the author and editor, who figures out what the art should look like and who should make it. A smart first step is to create a mood board. A mood board is a collection of existing images, pulled from the internet or other books and media, that explore and illustrate various styles and sensibilities. If the team decides they want watercolors, what should those paintings be like? Tightly rendered or washy, casual and light or more serious and arty, full scenes, close-ups, varied perspectives? Just like trying on dresses in front of a mirror, gathering images for a mood board helps clarify: Does this look right? What does this say? Is this what we're going for? Pulling images for a mood board often sparks new ideas and leads the team in ways they hadn't yet imagined.

How Many Images?

Working with images is its own part-time job—naming, organizing, storing, cropping, resizing, adjusting for color or contrast, cleaning up, and prepping for print. Not to mention laying them out on the page. I've worked on books with twelve images and books with two thousand. A book with a couple thousand photographs isn't only different to design than one with a dozen, it's much more work to manage.

The number of images should fit with the book's function and its budget. A book with step-by-step visual instructions—how to change your bike tire—might have a lot of little illustrations. For cookbooks, it's widely believed that people make only the recipes that are pictured, and authors often imagine that they will include a photo of every dish. This rarely happens: when images are commissioned for a book, every one comes with a dollar sign attached. How many images appear reflects how many the publisher (or author) is willing to pay for.

When images already exist, they need to be culled. Sometimes authors want to share everything they've ever made or photographed or collected on a subject. Editors and designers can help authors curate the selection for its greatest impact. Finally: page count. As noted earlier, page count is determined in an equation that balances the material at hand, the purpose of the book, and the book's budget. The number of images is directly tied to how many are going to fit between the covers.

Sample Design

Sample design is the vanilla term for what may be the hardest and most important (and most exciting) phase of book design, particularly for illustrated books. It's when a designer takes some portion of text and some portion of art and figures out what the book is going to look like and how it will work.

Design brings shape, structure, and pacing to a project. It's not unusual for authors to tell me that everything became so much clearer once they saw some portion of their manuscript in designed spreads. "Ah! That's what I've been doing!" Design can illuminate the relationship (or, at least, one possible relationship) between words and images that authors have suspected but haven't been quite able to grasp. When the text or images don't match up with the intentions of the book, it's in the design phase that this becomes obvious. Authors who have been picturing big, glorious images may realize that—to fit everything on the page—the images need to be smaller than hoped. At that point they may decide to cut or rework text, or beg their editor for more pages. It's hard to create a visually oriented book before you know how visuals will be oriented—an argument for creating sample design at the earliest realistic stage for such books.

Design brings not only structure, but also style. Type, color, ornamentation, and tone are worked out in this phase too. How the book ends up looking is an amalgam of so many factors: subject matter, audience, the look and feel and amount of the art, the size of the page, the kind of text, how it is structured, the length of the paragraphs, and the very words used. Designers integrate all that data and come back with ideas in the form of fonts, colors, and layouts. Of course there are always a thousand ways to go. In a complex book, sample design almost always involves some back-and-forth as structure and styles are revised, intentions clarified, and the ideas of author and designer find a mutually satisfying expression. (This back-and-forth can sometimes spiral out of control. Smart publishers have systems for making this process productive instead of frustrating.)

And keep this in mind (always, and particularly during sample design): design emerges from the *specifics* of the text and the art. What the author—or designer—wants is just the stepping-off point. You may love Ottolenghi's recipe design and envision that for your cookbook, but the length and structure and style of your recipes are different from his (let's hope). His design fits his work. The design of your book must fit yours.

Book Maps

But we're not done with prep just yet. Once sample design has been figured out, an art director, or sometimes the editor, will put together a book map, sketching out the flow and pace of the entire book based on the example of the sample design. You can't put the picture of the roast next to the recipe for the soufflé. Book maps help everyone get a handle on the mass of material—What goes where? How many pages do we need? Do we have that many pages?

Chronology, geography, taxonomy, category, or something else inside an author's head might determine a book's sequence. Designers will follow the editorial structure and do our best to make the puzzle pieces fit (or show where they will not fit). Sample design and book maps should result in rough but realistic word counts for pages, and page counts for sections or chapters. Unlike in other books, writing and editing text *to fit* is a common scenario when creating illustrated books. The better the sample design and book map, the better the word count estimates will be, and the less cutting will be needed in the layout phase.

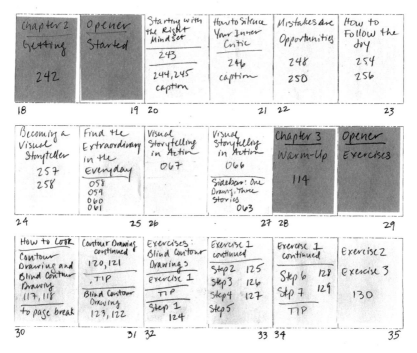

This section from a carefully planned book map sketches out where chapter openers, subheadings, sidebars, and images (indicated by numbers) will appear.

Designing Visual Books

In many ways, designing visual books is like other forms of graphic design. The design of a poster or an ad or the cover of an LP is also a matter of placing images and type together in a rectangle. The difference with books is that they're so long. It's like designing three hundred book covers in a row, a dozen magazines back-to-back. Every page must have an internal logic as well as relate to all the pages before and after. It takes a lot of control—administrative, aesthetic—to keep track of the many pieces and fit them together in a way that makes sense over hundreds of pages. And making sense matters only if readers care. Designers must make visual books not only clear and cohesive but interesting and appealing or they'll never make it out of the warehouse.

This is the underlying grid of this page, and this book.

The Grid

In a novel, it's pretty clear where the text is going to sit on the page. But in a visual book, many more, and varied, elements create a more complex page and different kind of puzzle. When there's no central text block, perhaps no primary text at all, how to decide what goes where? Enter the grid: the skeleton or framework of a book page (and most other things that are graphically designed).

Book designers divide their pages into rows and columns, creating an organizational system for the placement of text and images. A simple grid might have two or three columns and two or three rows. A more complex grid might have eight or more. In some grids, areas will be designated for specific use: this is the sidebar column, this is the body text column, the row at the top will hold images. Other layouts will be constructed so that text and image can hopscotch around, spanning multiple rows or columns. Images can be of different sizes and set in different places on the page. Some pages might be full of text, some have none at all, and others somewhere in between.

And here's a secret: *every* book page is designed with an underlying grid. For the simplest text pages, it just happens to be a very simple grid. More complex books must employ more complex and ingenious ones.

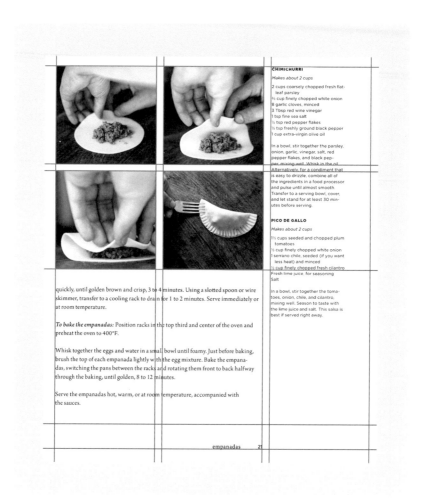

A book page with three (even) columns and four (uneven) rows.

Images

An illustrated book is a book with images, no matter what kind of images, including photographs. But *illustration* refers specifically to nonphotographic art, made by hand or digitally, and can be referred to by the shorthand term *illo* (like a photograph is a photo). Illustrated books can include illos or photos or both.

Illos that aren't embedded within a background are called spot art. Pick up a pencil and draw a flower. The flower, floating on your notepad with nothing around it, is spot art. Spot art is common in certain kinds of illustrated books—reference books, how-to books, some kids books—and its idiosyncratically edged, unbounded, nonsquareness allows it to interact with text intimately and dynamically. It can be sprinkled across a page, slid right up against the type, or even break into it. But most artwork—photographs, the *Mona Lisa*—isn't spot art but instead bound inside a rectangular frame. Books are rectangles filled with pages and pages of rectangles (text columns are rectangles too).

Spot art

What to do with rectangular art? How to keep it lively and interesting? The most obvious move is to make it big. Big images are exciting! Fill the entire page with an image, the frame disappears. It's *all* art. When art extends past the page edge it's called a bleed. Images can bleed on all sides or one, two, or three. Images can also be inset where their edges are visible. The image has a frame around it, which can give a tidy, contained look to a page. Small images can have their own drama if set within a lush expanse of negative space; profligate displays of emptiness are provocative and attention grabbing. Multiple images are usually placed in rows, columns, grids (sometimes asymmetrical grids[1]), not willy-nilly. Images sitting together

Not spot art

on the page are in a conversation scripted by the designer. Varying image size and placement and moving between pages with single images and pages with multiples creates rhythm and flow. Some books have a steady beat, others are more syncopated.

Setting images alongside blocks of text is part of the deal. Whether by choice or necessity, art and words often share the page. Starting with a suitable grid is the key to success here. Designers consider how much text, how many images, the width of the columns, the size of the art, what goes where, looking for balance and clarity. Images and text usually need plenty of elbow room.[2] When text and art are too close, it creates unwanted tension.

Placing Images

Inset

Full bleed

Cropped

If only Leonardo had left more room for text.

Room for text

I wish you could see this better.

Screened-back image

Distortions don't make good design.

In children's picture books—and some other kinds of books—type will overlay, or sit on top of, an image. Careful here! In this situation, art must be created deliberately with "room for text." That is, the illustrator (or sometimes a photographer) will be shown the space needed for text on each page so they can carve out quiet areas for type to sit. If there's no space reserved for text, the author might find their sentences plopped on top of a rainbow sky and neither the words nor the art will be entirely legible. Some designers will screen back images—that is, increase the transparency of a photo or illustration so type is more legible on top of it. To my eye, this is often a failure—compromising both image and type, insulting them both.

Another thing I don't do with images: distort them by stretching or smushing. While images, particularly photographs, are often cropped—sometimes for drama, more often for fit—cropping means adjusting the frame *around* an image, not adjusting the image inside the frame.

The other danger zone is the gutter. The binding of a book eats everything that crosses it. Designers are extra careful with art that spans the gutter, never placing important visual information there.

Type

In all book design, as I've already noted, type is styled to reflect hierarchy, function, and distinction—bold for this, italic for that. In visually oriented books this styling can be even *more*: more expressive, more decorative, more playful, more tonal. Larger pages offer possibilities. Color adds a whole other dimension. Text is often broken into smaller bites, a license to have more fun. The what and how of the material will push the vibe one way or another from the largest titles to the smallest captions.

Part of this is that there is more opportunity. Illustrated books might have fewer words than your typical text-driven books, but there are often more kinds of text. Cookbooks have headnotes and yields and pantry lists. Craft books have sets of numbered instructions, lists of materials, measurement tables. Art books might have essays, interviews, descriptions, and captions. Field guides and other reference books contain all manner of facts and information designed for quick scanning. It's not uncommon for illustrated books to include dozens of kinds of text, each needing its own set of features to define and clarify their relationships. Picking fonts is just step one. We've got a million fashion choices to consider: what size, what boldness, what alignment and spacing? Should this be roman or italic? *Semibold* italic? *Extra bold* italic? In all caps? Purple? Multiply this by ten or twenty or fifty—*each* kind of text will be thought through at this level and every detail is significant. It's the difference (well, *a* difference) between *Joy of Cooking* and the Snoop Dogg cookbook.

INGREDIENTS

FOR THE STREUSEL TOPPING
½ cup sugar

6 tablespoons all-purpose flour

2 tablespoons finely ground almond meal

Pinch of kosher or sea salt

2 tablespoons unsalted butter,
cut into small pieces

FOR THE CAKE
8 tablespoons (1 stick) unsalted butter at
room temperature, plus extra for the pan

1 cup all-purpose flour, plus extra for the pan

½ cup finely ground almond meal

[TIP] Cut a cartouche out of parchment paper
and use it to line the bottom of the pan.

Ingredients

For the Streusel Topping

½ cup sugar

6 tablespoons all-purpose flour

2 tablespoons finely ground almond meal

Pinch of kosher or sea salt

2 tablespoons unsalted butter, cut into
small pieces

For the Cake

8 tablespoons (1 stick) unsalted butter
at room temperature, plus extra for the pan

1 cup all-purpose flour, plus extra for the pan

½ cup finely ground almond meal

Tip Cut a cartouche out of parchment paper
and use it to line the bottom of the pan.

Here are two ways a designer might approach the same material.
Font choice, font styling, and the use of space are thought through and
deployed to express functionality, relationships, and voice.

Color

Books with images are often printed in color, and once you've secured
color printing, you can use it in all sorts of ways beyond the art: for type
or backgrounds, patterns, ornaments, frames, little spots or splashes.
It's amazing how a little color on a page brightens and enlivens things.
An empty page feels one way, while an empty *red* page is something
else entirely.

Designers, like painters, decide on an intentional and limited sets
of colors—their palette—and work within those. Color palettes are like
mood lighting, setting the tone for the party. Bright, saturated palettes
are a different mode from a group of light pastels or moody secondary
tones. Color palettes can be groups of complementary colors or deliberately contrasting hues or some combination of the two. They might
include three colors or ten. When color palettes get too large, they
become unwieldy.

When color is an option, neutral tones may feel like a wasted opportunity, but the opposite is true. Designers are always looking for light tones to use behind type, and pastels (bringing red, orange, blue, or green down to a light tint) can feel too cute, babyish, or inappropriate for some kinds of content. (Let's face it, pastels are often ugly.) I use light grays and warm, doughy whites over and over again in the books I design. A light yellow with or without a squirt of blue is bright without being cloying. Neutrals differentiate without needing to assert too much personality. They don't compete with imagery. In full-color books, with bright white paper, even a subtle tonal difference from the page is clear to a reader and can delineate a sidebar or other text area without being intrusive.

Adding color to type can be magic. When I set my A-heads in red, I don't need to do much more to distinguish them from the rest of the text. Here's where I do indulge bright and saturated color so it stands out from the mostly black type. I love to use color as a highlight for elements like chapter numbers, running feet, page numbers, or for occasional emphasis like "serving size" in a cookbook or "tip" in a how-to. But I don't set body copy in color. Long passages of text that aren't printed in black, or another very dark and contrasting color, are irritating to read. Small type can run into color alignment, or registration, issues when printing, and designers create color palettes with this in mind. Designers call white text on a dark background reversed or "knocked out." When knocked-out type gets too small, the surrounding ink can encroach.

But even in full-color, illustrated books, sometimes all the type must be kept black. This is both good news and bad news. The good news is that it usually means the publisher has hopes of selling the book in translation. If all the type is black, there is only one ink plate (in a CMYK setup) that will need to be changed. Everything in color remains; the black type is lifted out and replaced with the translated text. The bad news is, of course, all the type is black.

Finally, when working in a book with full-color images, I'm careful not to get in their way by using *too* much color elsewhere. Keeping other elements quiet around images allows them the space and attention they deserve.

Image Quality and Production

When working on physical books, designers must always keep in mind how things will actually print. Getting the paper-and-ink book to reflect the version on the screen, or in the designer's or author's head, requires its own expertise. Publishers who specialize in illustrated books make sure they have the staff, budget, and timeline to make it happen. This can mean production directors who work directly with printers; rounds of color proofs (which take time and money); and art directors and designers who understand the possibilities and limitations of printing and can speak its language.

Full-color books are often printed in Asia and Europe, where printers are set up for the more elaborate manufacturing these books require, and communicating with overseas printers and shipping boxes of books across the ocean adds time and complexity to the process. When printing overseas, publishers usually add three to four months to the schedule to account for transport and customs. In recent years, supply-chain issues have made printing "offshore" less attractive, and publishers have scrambled to find North American printers who can do the work affordably. Keeping printing closer to its ultimate distribution is a more environmentally responsible move as well.

Printing in color is delicate, as anyone who has had their holiday cards printed knows. What you see on your screen and what comes back from the printer aren't necessarily the same. At minimum, every image should be of print-quality resolution (commonly called high resolution, or high res) with adequate focus and contrast. If your only image of a rare mushroom is the one you took in the rain at twilight on your cell phone, and it's not clear if it's a mushroom or your foot—friend, leave it out. Low-quality images undermine a book's authority and are distracting and unpleasant for readers.

Even with high-quality images, it's common for printed images to look darker than they appear on the screen (where they're made up of light rather than ink). Color and tonality is sometimes horribly off. Printing full pages of color (called floods), such a beloved design move, is particularly chancy with digital printing where ink coverage can be inconsistent and "banding" is a common, unwanted phenomenon. Not only process but paper choice makes a difference here—the pleasure of a toothy uncoated page might be mitigated by how dull images appear as the ink soaks into the grain. Generally speaking, bright white, coated papers show images best.

The reproduction of fine art brings its own host of concerns, including the photographing of artwork—a medium layered on top of a medium—and extra attention to color and clarity. Comparing the reproduction of art with its original is the most demanding kind of proofing. Making sure that food looks appetizing is another area where careful color proofing is essential. No one wants the chicken looking a little blue. I've worked on many books that use historic photography, almost all of which comes speckled and scratched and must be painstakingly cleaned up and retouched. In books where image quality is of utmost importance, publishers will often send art to a photo lab or other professional whose job is to prep the files for the best printed results (professional photographers will often do this themselves).

Once files have been sent to the printer, there's often a lot of high-fiving and congratulatory emails. The project feels, finally, over. But it's not! Vision, planning, cool art, great ideas, and sharp design will all go to waste if the printing and production is weak. For illustrated books, publishers should always work with high-quality, hard-copy color proofs for an accurate reflection of the printed result. If you're self-publishing, be sure to order a hard-copy proof version of your book. Working with printers and keeping attention focused through proofing stages is as important as any other phase in the process. The finished book should be a beauty, and not a surprise.

Chapter 6
Ebooks

At an early ebook conference in 1999, Dick Brass of Microsoft predicted that we were on the verge of a radical shift in reading: by 2018, he said, 90 percent of all books sold would be ebooks.[1] Uh, not quite. A quarter of a century after this misjudgment, ebooks are somewhere in the realm of 15 to 20 percent of the (trackable) book market.[2] Many people now read (or "read") in both digital (including audiobooks) and print formats, swapping between presentations depending on circumstance and the book in question.[3]

Each format has its bragging rights. Paper-and-ink books are tested by two thousand years of successful use and inhabit a physical and cultural aura that is hard to match. Audiobooks let us experience books while walking the dog, doing the dishes, or driving cross-country. They have the added pleasure of letting us hear the author (or a skilled voice actor) bring words to life. Ebooks can flaunt reader customization and accessibility features. They come with their own dictionary, can be had in the click of a mouse, and require no shipping or storage. You can walk around town with every book you've read in the past year in your pocket.

Audiobooks leave little work for a visual designer—we reconfigure the cover into a square for display in the online store and our work is done. (That square probably refers to the shape of CDs or even LPs, the first formats for audiobooks.) Ebook designers have a few more obstacles to contend with. Aside from understanding typography and hierarchy, they must tangle with the complexities of computer language and the habits of individual readers, whose preferences may interact with (and change) a designer's intentions. They also must bow to the proclivities of the devices themselves, and the software running on them. Ebook design is just learning to walk. There's a lot of growth still to come.

Brief History

In 1971 a college student named Michael S. Hart typed the United States' Declaration of Independence into a computer at the University of Illinois. His idea was to digitize and make available ten thousand of the most popular books in the world, free to the public, as digital files. (He typed the first three hundred of these in by hand himself, including the King James Bible and the works of Homer.) This endeavor, named Project Gutenberg after the progenitor of the printed book, is considered the first digital library and is still around, now with over sixty thousand titles available as free downloadable ebooks. These earliest digital books were heavy on the digital and light on the book. They weren't the shape of a book or the size of the book and they didn't have the markers of the book page—margins framing a contained column of justified text. In fact, Hart deliberately used as little formatting as possible so the files could be accessed in as many ways as possible. What distinguished them as "books" is that they had existed previously as books.

Project Gutenberg began in the world of mainframe computers, but by the 1990s regular people owned personal computers and early ebooks became available on floppy disks and eventually CD-ROMs. Understanding that for widespread use books need to be able to be held in hand (no one wants to read Jane Austen while sitting at their desk), Sony developed the first e-reader, the Data Discman, in 1992. With this device, which looked like a cross between a flip phone and a VCR, you could feed a CD-ROM into one end, press the play button, and read the text on 2½-inch screen. The Data Discman included a mini (physical) keyboard for search capabilities. You probably don't remember the Data Discman and the other failed attempts at e-readers that followed. Perhaps slightly more successful was software developed for reading books on the popular handheld computer of the time, the Palm Pilot.[4]

But the small selection of available titles kept the adoption of ebooks at a trickle. Eventually Amazon stomped in, overturning the flowerpots. In 2007, Amazon released the Kindle e-reader and launched Kindle Direct Publishing, which allowed *any* user to upload a book to sell on the site. In one fell swoop, ebooks and self-publishing became significant market forces. (The iPhone also came out in 2007, creating another potential platform for ebooks.) Unlike Sony and others before it, Amazon already had weight with publishers and could push for the hottest books to be released as ebooks. They also had the eyeballs of book buyers and would advertise "Start reading *The Hunger Games* on your Kindle in under a minute" on the same web page where people were already shopping for the print version. Amazon sold ebooks at low, low prices, setting off a yearslong battle with publishers over pricing.[5] And, with the Kindle, Amazon had created a handheld device that didn't altogether compromise the pleasure of reading. In November 2007, *Newsweek* ran Jeff Bezos on the cover with the title "Books Aren't Dead, They're Just Going Digital."

The rise of ebooks was scary to some in the publishing world (and some in the reading world too).[6] Amazon has worked to harden the expectation that an ebook is cheaper than print, threatening publishers' profits. Free and cheap titles are still part of the ebook's appeal and Amazon's strategy.[7] But more, the idea that ebooks could replace printed books altogether felt, to some, like an existential threat—not only to the publishing industry but to our shared cultural history. The bound paper-and-ink book is a symbol of humanity's collected ideas and knowledge. The idea that our bookshelves would disappear into the ethereal realm of the digital, like so much else, felt like an impending loss. The writer Annie Proulx is quoted as saying, "Nobody is going to sit down and read a novel on a twitchy little screen. Ever."[8]

Well. The situation we find ourselves in is one in which print and ebooks (and audiobooks) present a range of reading choices that manage to coexist surprisingly comfortably. Ebooks have thrived in certain corners of publishing (most notably genre fiction) and barely make a dent in others (particularly illustrated books). They have a special relationship to the world of self-publishing, where freedom from the complexities of printing and storage has made them the format of choice for authors working the market on their own. And the ubiquity of book-sized (or smaller) personal devices—phones and tablets—have made adoption of ebooks make sense for a wide audience.

In *Book Wars*, John B. Thompson argues that ebooks have emerged as a new publishing *format*—much like the paperback, which was radical when it was first introduced too—but not a new *form*. As such, they can coexist inside the larger publishing ecosystem without dismantling it.[9] The writer and actor Stephen Fry noted, "One technology doesn't replace another, it complements. Books are no more threatened by Kindle than stairs by elevators."[10] Tell it to the pay phones.

Devices and Apps

An ebook is a computer file, written in a computer language, and human readers need a translator to access it. Glance around a subway or airport and you can see people reading on their phones, e-readers, and tablets. Students, journalists, scientists, and writers read books on their laptop and desktop computers. The physicality of our books— their size, heft, and materials—are, for many of us, part of their appeal (or at least what we're used to), and the devices and apps we use for ebooks have to work to mimic those qualities.

Dedicated e-readers are highly designed objects, attuned to people's reading habits and preferences. Their size, weight, materials, and finish, how square or rounded the corners, where the buttons go, are all design concerns that have been thought through in detail. (Just like designers of print books think through these questions in detail. Except the part about the buttons.) Screen technology has worked hard to meet the standards of print books (you can use e-reader screens in bright sun) and then raise them one (*and* in the dark). In online forums, boosters cheer for their various teams. ("Absolutely love the Kobo Libre, it's better than the Kindle Oasis and here's 1000 words on why.") There's a lot of scrutiny of and loyalty to e-reading devices because they're the container not for a single book but for— conceivably—all the books a person might read over a year or five years. They don't shapeshift to accommodate the particularities of a text and they're not handed down as law from publisher to reader. The user gets to pick how they like their books, although, once chosen, all books are going to squeeze into that same dress.

Even so, the popularity of dedicated e-readers is falling.[11] People already own phones and tablets and they read ebooks on those. So each book comes in the same wrapper as not only every other book but also your newspaper, email, social media feed, Netflix, and Wordle. Books are as easily accessible as everything else but similarly undistinguished.

And then there are the apps: Apple Books, Kindle, Kobo, Google; there are dozens of choices for e-reading apps, each with their own logic, features, and limitations. Readers will have preferences based on functionality, familiarity, and their feelings about Amazon. Each app operates a little differently. Do I tap or swipe? Is there the option to scroll? What are my choices for fonts? For size? For alignment? Can I see a thumbnail view? Do footnotes hyperlink or pop up? How is the dictionary viewed? Where do my notes go? The ebook experience is designed, largely, by industrial and software designers, not the person formatting the chapter heads for your individual title. It's a notable difference from the manufacture of printed books, where it's the publishing team, the people closest to the book, who are making the choices around a book's design and mechanics.

Reflowable Ebooks

There are two varieties of ebook: fixed layout and reflowable. Reflowable is the more common, by far, and what you probably imagine when you think of an ebook. It's right in the name: reflowable ebooks flow like water through a riverbed, filling the space as the water gets higher or lower and the banks widen or narrow. Designers (mostly) can't control this flow; when readers change the size of the text, the size of the screen, or the orientation of the screen—from profile to landscape—what's visible on any given page will change as well.

It is no coincidence that the energy in the ebook market is centered on fiction (romance is the biggest-selling category of ebooks by a significant margin[12]): reflowable ebooks work best for books that are text-focused. Books that rely on images or a tightly controlled relationship of elements to each other aren't as well suited to this format.

An advantage of reflowable ebooks is that the reader has this control over their presentation: the size of the type, what font, the alignment of the text can be adjusted to taste, or necessity for readers with low vision, within limits imposed by the device. "In ebooks, you have this tension, between the purity of a book's layout as it was envisioned in print, and the flexibility that e-reading brings to a customer, by allowing you to increase font size, read books across multiple devices, and so on," says Dave Limp of Amazon, "It's a tension between the beautiful but static nature of print, and the dynamism of digital."[13]

Much of the work of print designers is to nip and tuck every page, making sure each spread is its own perfect tableau. In ebooks, text runs wild and free. For designers, this a dramatic relinquishing of control. Justification, line breaks, a pretty rag along the right margin? Pffft. Widows and orphans are going to exist, passages of text get beheaded, tables split midrow. But even within this more limited environment, the designer's choices still matter. "Users want to retain control over their own experiences [but] also want their experiences to be guided and clear," said Khoi Vinh, a designer at Adobe, in a talk on the future of ebooks in 2007.[14] Conscientious designers understand the important differences between print and digital formats, design separate files for each, and adjust their design to each format's capabilities.

Another area of growth for ebooks is the academic market, and you can easily imagine the advantages: not needing to lug a bunch of twenty-pound textbooks around campus all day, for one. Digital textbooks also tend to be less expensive, eminently searchable, sometimes interactive, and easily had. On the other hand, textbooks are usually long and complex works with a lot of intricate page design. How successfully the material translates to a reflowable format will depend on informed decisions on the editorial level and strong work on the design side.

Fonts

There are some great screen fonts, and ebook designers enjoy choosing ones that feel like a match with a text. But devices and apps come loaded with default fonts, and designers need to weigh the pros and cons of embedding their own preferred fonts in an EPUB (EPUB, short for *electronic publication*, is the standard file type for ebooks). On the pro side, chosen fonts are chosen for a reason. Books are aesthetic objects, and type choice does a lot of work to reinforce tone and create beauty and clarity. Font selection is a fundamental part of book design, and surrendering it feels a little like neglect. Designers working with non-English words (even within a mostly English-language book) may decide to embed a font with a larger non-Latin character set. Non-Latin characters (or even less-common Latin characters) sometimes will not display with the default fonts loaded on a device and you'll end up with a sad empty box where the character belongs.

On the con side, embedded fonts can be expensive and complicated to license (although Google, for one, offers free web fonts that can be used for ebooks). All platforms will not receive embedded fonts with equal grace, some displaying them incorrectly or ignoring them altogether. Finally, for most books, the highly developed screen fonts that retailers have created to work with their devices and apps work well. Why fuss?

Typography

Ebooks that are being published alongside print versions (which are usually designed first) will follow in their typographic footsteps as much as possible. But ebooks must also be typeset to their own strengths and limitations and shouldn't adhere to conventions of printed book pages that don't make sense for the format.

As discussed in the earlier chapters, while designing for print, designers can explore a deep cache of type fashion. Ebook styling, on the other hand, should be lean and mean: bold, italic, caps. It's not that other styling isn't possible—it is—but it's unreliable. Small caps will show up as small caps in some places and not in others. Drop caps, so beloved by some authors, are buggy and full of surprises in different environments. Extra light, extra bold, extended or condensed fonts, text numerals, ligatures, and alternate characters may or may not appear as intended. I wouldn't risk it.

What designers cannot control in an ebook: the page size, the page margins, the font size, the font choice, text flow from line to line and from page to page. Ouch. Still, ebooks designed by skilled designers will be more polished and readable than those that are not. Designers *can* control how different types of text relate to each other through proportional sizing and spacing. And in-the-know designers make choices that make ebooks pleasant—setting body text left aligned (not justified) to avoid a sea of gappy lines, and turning off hyphenation, which can become chaotic and nonsensical outside of the watchful eye of a designer.

ALL YOU NEED TO KNOW ABOUT SELF-PUBLISH-ING

This is the kind of really ugly typography that shows up all over ebooks. Designers can prevent the worst offenses—in this instance, by using nonbreaking spaces in titles and turning off hyphenation throughout.

You know that chapter breaks give authors and readers an important editorial and psychological breather. In ebooks, designers bring personality to chapter designs but within a simpler framework that will look good on any screen. Making sure that chapters and other important dividers in the text begin on a new screen—not a given in an ebook—is an important part of shaping the book and creating hierarchy and clarity for readers.

Tables, the workhorse of the nonfiction book, are all kinds of messy for ebooks. A wide table with many columns can overhang the screen, forcing readers to scroll sideways to get all the information. Tables can break across pages and screens willy-nilly, even mid-row. Tables with complex styling of rows, columns, and cells may look correct on one device and amiss on another. Most ebook designers take care to create very simple tables even if this means reformatting them from a print book or manuscript. In some cases, converting tables to simpler bullet lists or placing them as "images" is a good solution to the table problem.

Images

Images are irrelevant to some books and absolutely integral to others. For those in which they're important, reflowable ebooks aren't the way to go. They simply don't handle well—by size or design—a visually focused, illustration-heavy book. For books where images don't appear: great! Reflowable ebooks are a good fit. But what to do about the ones in between? Text-driven books may use images occasionally or even often (like this one). Textbooks are full of text and also illustrations, tables, charts, and diagrams. Cookbooks may be design-driven but may also benefit from the wider availability that comes from being packaged as a reflowable ebook.

Reflowable ebooks are basically long vertical scrolls, and images will mostly fall above or below text in a single, continuous column (if all the images in an ebook are ganged at the end of the chapter, the designer has not set up their file correctly). A more dynamic relationship between images and text isn't possible (or not reliably, at least). Color—so precious and expensive in print—is free in ebooks. But not all devices display color—e-ink readers like Kindles and Kobos don't—adding yet another variable with which designers must contend.

As with all computer files, the size of ebooks affects how quickly they can be downloaded and how much space they consume on a device. Images add weight to an ebook, and some retailers have escalating fees for the file size of an ebook (Amazon charges by the megabyte for the most common royalty configuration). Editors and authors should weigh the value of images versus these factors, and designers should always optimize their image files to be as small as possible while retaining high-quality resolution.

Navigation

We navigate a printed book so easily, leafing through pages, opening to the middle or closer to the front or back, and sticking our thumb into the binding to save our place as we flip around. Navigating an ebook is more awkward. It's clear why the codex became more popular than the scroll. Still, software makers have worked hard to create systems that mimic the easy functionality of a physical book. Some things you can do: fast-forward from chapter to chapter, use thumbnail views to skim chapters or sections, use flip back buttons to bring you right back to specific spots (basically, a digital thumb), and add bookmarks—as many as you want. These features are designed as part of a device or app and are outside of the control of an individual designer.

Hyperlinks are a way that readers cruise all sorts of digital text, and ebooks rely on them to move you around the book.[15] The hyperlinked table of contents that appears in every ebook (even fiction) will pop you over to any place in a text. Hyperlinked footnotes keep the rest of the page neat and focused. Linked cross-references inside the book let the reader easily bop around. And links that point outside a book—to a dictionary, Wikipedia, or websites—will look up unfamiliar words, bring in additional information, and connect a text to the larger world. For designers, managing in-book and out-of-book hyperlinks is part of making a functioning reading experience.

Semantic Tagging

Ebook designers pay as much attention to how computers will read their books as to how humans will. Ebooks are coded in the computer language XHTML, and designers use tags to tell a device the function of each piece of text. Word processing programs also use tags; Microsoft Word calls them styles. In Word, you can designate a heading 1, a heading 2, a quote, a list, a title, or an emphasis. A writer might style their heading 1 as 24-point Times New Roman bold, and when the file comes to the designer, the designer may change that to 18-point Helvetica Regular. No matter, the function of the text remains: this is a first-level heading. This is called semantic tagging and it's how designers in both print and ebooks work on their files and, generally speaking, how computers understand the text as well.

Accessibility features are an important attribute of ebooks—allowing low-vision readers who have trouble with print to access material in other ways. Semantic tags allow computers to translate text meaningfully for features like text-to-speech and braille output. A computer translating the structure of a book to a vision-impaired reader can let them know when they come to a heading or a sidebar, for instance, or it can emphasize words that are tagged "emphasis" appropriately. Semantic tags are also used by search engines, which can see what text is a heading, what is a sidebar, and so on, and use that intelligently in search results.[16]

Images are also tagged in ebooks, with an alt tag that alerts the computer—"here's an image"—and contains alt text ("alternative text"), a description that the computer can then read aloud. A photo of a lotus might be tagged "a pink lotus floating in a pond in a Japanese garden." A vision-impaired reader using text-to-speech will then be able to listen to the description and understand the content. And the device itself now knows what this image is and can use that information in its search functions. Alt text should be considered part of the text of the book (by editors and authors), the same way visible captions are, and similarly taken into account: it should be useful, age appropriate, and not overly generic or redundant.

Questions around tagging of both words and images can fall between the cracks as a text travels between editorial and design. Editors and authors sometimes ignore this important phase, leaving it to designers to encode text properly. It's like sending a manuscript to the designer before it has been copyedited. In a world in which documents move from the author's or editor's Word file to the designer's InDesign file to the ebook designer's EPUB files, a text should carry its tags along with it like luggage so that everyone who encounters it can understand what's what. Editors should control that process—and the editorial consequences of it—by tagging manuscripts before they go to design. See more about where tagging fits in the design process on page 179.

Testing

All designers proof their work before they send it out into the world. For print designers, this usually means looking at digital or hard-copy proofs sent by the printer and, if everything looks as it should, giving a green light with the confidence that the result will emerge as expected. (The infelicities of print on demand destabilize this system somewhat.) For ebook designers, proofing or testing requires a more varied approach. Many ebook designers own an assortment of e-readers, including a multigenerational array of Kindles, Kobos, and Nooks. They will also open and scroll through their books on the most popular apps on phones and tablets and personal computers. It's not uncommon for books to look good and work right on some devices but be unpleasantly surprising on others. Working out the kinks can be a process of stripping the design elements down to bare bones. If the goal is to make the book readable on as many screens as possible, including older devices, a lowest-common-denominator solution is often where ebook designers find themselves.[17]

Fixed-Layout Ebooks

The second variety of ebook, the fixed-layout ebook, has the strengths of both digital and print books. It can include animation, image galleries, reader interactivity, video, narration, and other audio elements. Text is "live," so, just as in any ebook, it can be selected, searched, and hyperlinked. But text doesn't reflow, so the designer-determined positioning of images and the choices around type design are (mostly) retained. These books can look gorgeous and do so much. Really, what more could you ask for?

And yet fixed-layout ebooks have failed to take the world by storm.[18] Turns out most people buy and read straightforward, text-driven, reflowable ebooks.[19] One statistic I read reported that fixed-layout ebooks made up less than 1 percent of the commercial ebook market.[20] The lack of reader customization, while good for the *look* of these books, can be annoying to digital readers used to bumping up the type size. The fixedness of their layout can make them next to impossible to enjoy on the smallest screens.

Image-driven books, the most natural content for fixed-layout ebooks, tend also to be ones where the physicality of the object is the most important. Few people want to read to their child at bedtime from a computer screen. There's no setting these out on the coffee table or displaying them on the cookbook shelf in your kitchen. As John B. Thompson writes, "Ebooks make terrible gifts."[21] And while you can view a fixed-layout ebook on a tablet or phone, Kindles will not display them, cutting off a sizable audience of ebook devotees. (Kindle offers a proprietary format for children's picture books and comics, basically telling the publishing world, "Don't bother with fixed-layout ebooks in other categories.")

Designing for fixed-layout ebooks is pretty similar to designing for print. All the rules of typography and spatial relationships apply (and will *mostly* appear as desired on *most* devices). But there's a crucial difference: the spread. Spreads are innate to the function of the codex but a skeuomorphism in a digital book. That is, presenting an ebook in spreads is a purely symbolic nod toward its earlier incarnation. Spreads aren't useful in an ebook—perhaps are even an obstacle, forcing readers into landscape view—and, thus, should be abandoned. However, if a design-forward book began its life in print, reworking for a single-page view can easily become a full-on redesign.

The addition of multimedia effects such as added audio, animation, or video also must be created (by the designer or someone else), integrated, and tested. This may be a significant layering on of material, and technical challenges, the designer will need to address. Copious testing across devices is recommended.

• • •

When the idea of digital books first emerged, there was a sense that this new format could deliver something that was "more than a book." Visions of technological innovation beckoned: Children's books that would read aloud, highlighting the words as they go. Cookbooks with pop-up videos that showed specific techniques in detail. Textbooks that came loaded with interactive problem sets at the end of every chapter. All these things can be, and have been, done. And yet print still thrives, and the ebook market is dominated by text-driven ebooks with few bells and whistles. Is that because *readers* aren't interested in "enhanced" books or because *publishers* have not been particularly interested in creating them? Has it been the result of lousy PR that leaves readers asking, Where can I find such books? How do I access them on my device? What makes them different from a website other than I have to pay for them? Perhaps, as one writer surmised, "Reading is a technology that works. And it works in part by immersing the reader in the text itself. The lack of video / music . . . [isn't] a problem to solve. The lack of those things is the feature."[22]

That said, our idea of what books are, and what they do, *has* evolved. The initial shock has worn off and digital books are an everyday part of the publishing landscape. At Amazon, the ebook and audiobook buttons sit right next to the hardcover and paperback choices and no one bats an eye. Can the "enhanced" book ever join the club? (Is it Amazon, ultimately, that is preventing it from doing so?) At some point, will the combination of ever-advancing technology, smart editorial ideas, and useful, elegant design make some form of enhanced book irresistible, for both publishers and readers? At least for some categories— textbooks and reference being the most likely—it's a good bet.[23]

The STUFF of DREAMS

OUR HOPES FOR A BETTER FUTURE

BILL SPEAR

Chapter 7

The Design Process

Up to this point, I've focused on the book as an object and what designers think about as they work. But this creative process exists within a larger publishing process that includes editors and copyeditors and art directors and marketing folks and, of course, authors. How does it all fit together? In this chapter I'm going to walk through the general stages of the design process as it plays out within traditional publishing or for authors who are self-publishing.

Books have two design phases—cover design and interior design—each with its own demands, schedule, and, sometimes, staff. For authors working with a publishing house, both phases can be (unnecessarily) mysterious. Oftentimes the stages and timeline aren't explained to authors. Your cover may be sprung on you while in the middle of copyediting your manuscript, without your realizing that the process had even begun. The discussion that follows should give you some sense of orientation and empowerment. On the other end of the spectrum, authors who are self-publishing may find they know a lot less about design than they thought. Forget designing your own cover, art-directing it will be a big enough challenge. The information here is meant to give you some basic footing in finding and directing a designer.

The design process is thrilling—and scary—because it represents a new phase. Not only are other people reading your book, but they're making decisions about how it will be presented to the world. There's another language—a visual language—set on top of your own. As the novelist Jhumpa Lahiri writes, "This moment teaches me to let go of the book. It signifies a loss of control."[1] Think of it this way: manuscripts live in your mind and on your computer, but *books* exist out in the world. They're no longer simply yours.

Traditional Publishing

Authors working with a traditional publishing house have made a deal. Literally. A "book deal": you give me this, I'll give you that. One of the things the author *gets* in a book deal is the professional design of their book and cover. Something the author forfeits is complete control over that process.

How the design process goes depends a lot on who is publishing and some on who is being published. The big houses have more resources and reach (and status). But the entrenched and oddly siloed systems around design at big publishers can keep authors at arm's length. Midsize and small presses may offer more opportunity for author contribution and collaboration, although of course it varies from press to press.

Many authors, particularly new authors, are so grateful to have their books published that they feel they can't speak up or give feedback on the design of their book. Some authors may feel unclear about what is occurring in-house or what part they're meant to play in this phase. Other authors are micromanagers (or divas), trying to exert an inappropriate level of control regarding design. The best design process won't ignore authors or appease them. Instead, it keeps them informed and respects their insight while maintaining confident authority over strategy, direction, and craft.

The Design Team

There is a big difference between a staff of a thousand and one of eight, and the difference will trickle down to how a book is designed, who works on what, and who talks to whom. The design team is structured differently depending on the size of the publishing house, their in-house workflows, and the design complexity of a book. At many presses the primary contact for the author is their editor, and design ideas and feedback will funnel through that person. At others, the art director may step in when cover design begins. It isn't uncommon for the person who designs your cover to be different from the person who designs your interior. It is also not uncommon for authors to have little or no contact with anyone designing any part of their book. These are the people who may be involved in the design of a book, along with their common job titles.

Creative director. The head honcho, keeping an eye on everything going on visually with a publisher's list, which includes book and cover design as well as marketing and promotional campaigns.

Art director. The lynchpin. The AD assigns designers for both covers and interiors; contributes to (and often manages) and communicates the design brief; creates and tracks the design/production schedule; works with the production side to develop specs (in smaller houses there may be no production person and the AD is the contact with the printer); ferries design rounds between designer, editor, author, and proofreader; and is the primary contact between those parties. In some houses this position has the title design director or design manager rather than art director. Many houses have multiple art directors, but your book will have only one.

Designer/cover designer. This person might design your cover or your entire book, depending on the setup at the publishing house and the kind of book you've written. They can be in-house or freelance. They consult with, get direction from, and give designs to the art director.

Production manager. This person takes the specs for a book and finds the right printer at the right cost. They let the rest of the team know what is financially realistic and what is available in terms of materials, processes, and printing effects. They're the primary contact with the printer (or printer's representative, called a print broker) and keep track of the proofing process and printing and delivery timelines.

Lines of Communication

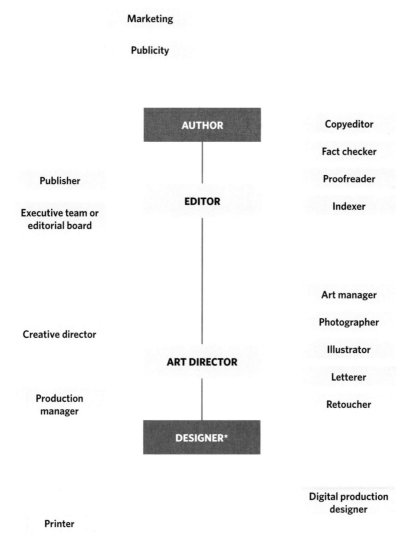

Sales

Marketing

Publicity

| | AUTHOR | Copyeditor |

AUTHOR

Copyeditor

Fact checker

Publisher

Proofreader

EDITOR

Executive team or
editorial board

Indexer

Art manager

Photographer

Creative director

Illustrator

ART DIRECTOR

Letterer

Production
manager

Retoucher

DESIGNER*

Digital production
designer

Printer

This is a general outline of who talks to whom during the design and production process.
Every publishing house is structured a little (or maybe significantly) differently.

*Or cover designer + interior designer/compositor

Compositor/typesetter. In projects not typeset by the designer, the compositor completes the interior layout. Working with a template created by a designer, or a standard template used by a publisher, they pour the full manuscript and complete the page design. This is a high-skilled job, and many art directors rely on trusted compositors (in-house or freelance) to manage the idiosyncrasies and unanticipated issues that are bound to arise when working through an entire book.

Digital production designer. In most publishing houses, ebook formatting is created in a digital production department or outsourced to a service provider (that is, it isn't completed by the designer of the printed book). While the designer of the ebook isn't usually part of developing the cover or print design, they have the responsibility of making the digital version of the text look good and work right.

Editor. While *not* a member of the design team, the editor is intimately involved in the design process. They're the gatekeeper, the aperture through which all communication flows, the advocate for both author and press. In many houses, there is more than one editor on a title—the acquisitions editor who brings the project to the press, interacts with the editorial board, and shepherds it through development and then a project editor, or manuscript editor, who takes it from there, managing the stages of copyediting, proofreading, fact-checking (when needed), and indexing (again, when needed).

The Cover Design Process

The cover design process is sometimes a breeze and sometimes a trial. The kind of book it is, the conventions at each publishing house, the personalities of the folks on the team, the personality of the author, the length of the schedule, the experience of the designer, and how big or ambitious the book is perceived to be all contribute to how the cover process plays out and whether everyone is elated or exhausted at the end. The flowchart on page 173 shows general, or possible, routes for a cover design to travel. Note the spots where design is in danger of getting sucked into an infinity loop of feedback and revision.

Engaging the Author

Effective editors engage their authors early in the design process and are sincerely interested in their thoughts. Many publishers use a questionnaire to elicit the author's ideas, and that information, often verbatim, will end up in the cover brief given to the designer. Authors are sometimes invited in (or to a call) to meet the design and marketing teams in advance of cover design. (Authors can ask for a call with their editor and art director if one isn't offered, though publishers' practices on this point may vary.) Authors who are recruited into the process and feel like part of the team are more likely to *act* like part of the team. Authors who are ignored as initial concepts develop can get in a defensive crouch or feel like they must argue, contradict, or micromanage in order to feel some ownership.

Launch

In most publishing houses, there is an initial cover launch meeting where the publishing team will talk through the positioning and possible cover direction for each title. This is the point where anything is possible, and the team can think broadly and imaginatively about how a book might present itself to the world. The

Cover Design Process

Internal launch

Design brief

Designer assigned

Initial cover designs

In-house
feedback

repeat, as needed

Revision

Cover design(s)
shared with author

Author
feedback

repeat, as needed

Revision

Cover choice shared
with sales team,
buyers, distributors,
etc.

Possibly more
feedback

repeat, as needed

Revision

Final front cover

author's thoughts will be shared by the editor at this meeting. The ideas that rise to the top will make it into the design brief (see page 66) and on to the designer.

Initial Cover Designs

Designers typically are given two to three weeks for initial cover designs and are expected to show at least three distinct approaches (though different publishers will have different instructions). As I described in chapter 3, these first concepts should respond to the direction given in the brief and will usually include some other, unexpected ideas as well. Presenting a variety of approaches is important so that the rest of the team can understand what feels like a fit.

In-House Feedback

There's going to be feedback. Most cover designs go through a number of rounds (and some go through a lot) as designers are asked for iterations, explorations, changes. In many cases, the art director and designer work together for a round or two to hone designs before sharing even with the larger in-house team. What's working, or how an idea might be tweaked to work better, isn't always clear. What's *not* working usually is, and those ideas—and the hours spent developing them—are quickly tossed aside. Sigh.

In-house requests for changes are usually along the lines of "Can you strengthen the type for the author name?" or "We like cover 3 but would you try a different background?" although they can, on occasion, get very specific: "How about a clover rather than a thistle on cover 1?" It's good for authors to realize that the first cover(s) they see aren't (usually) the actual first cover ideas. Having revised and winnowed, the publishing team will have some investment in the covers they present to the author and believe that what they're showing is strong.

Author Feedback

Sending the cover to an author is a delicate moment, obviously, and the editor (or art director, in some cases) can set the mood by providing context for what they're presenting. It isn't enough to say, "Everyone here loves this cover!" and hope for the best. If the editor (or art director) believes in a certain approach, they should explain *why* it works. Whether or not they're explicitly asked, authors can give feedback on the cover(s) they're shown.

Most traditionally published authors are given the right to "cover consultation," but not "cover approval," in their contract. This means the publisher will make the final call. But publishers really don't want their authors to be unhappy. They know that the author is the single strongest advocate for the book and that an author who feels crummy about their cover will be less likely to be posting it three times a day on Instagram. They expect to hear from you.

You are more likely to end up with an awesome cover if you stay focused on the big picture. If you don't understand why you should leave the details of typography and layout to the design team, please go back and reread this entire book. Here are some suggestions for responding effectively to cover design.

Do a vibe check. On a macro level, does it feel right? Authors are fine-tuned to the energy and atmosphere of their book and often intuit when a cover isn't quite nailing the vibe: "It feels quiet, when it should feel joyous." "It looks retro when it's not retro." "It comes off as self-help when it should be more memoir." Authors also know their content, intimately, and can point out any factual misses that make it onto cover concepts: "You put a rainbow trout on the cover when it needs to be an Atlantic trout." "The story is set in the 1970s but that font says 1960s to me." "Um, this book is set in Jerusalem and that's a photo of Tel Aviv."

Respond, don't solve. One of Neil Gaiman's rules for writing applies here: "Remember: when people tell you something's wrong or doesn't work for them, they are almost always right. When they tell you exactly what they think is wrong and how to fix it, they are almost always wrong."[2] To put it another way: your reaction is welcome, your art direction is not.

Once I was working on a cover that included two author names. I had set the whole line in all caps: BOB WOODWARD AND CARL BERNSTEIN (it wasn't really them). The authors came back and asked for the "and" to be an ampersand, then in another font, then in small caps. None of these changes looked quite right. Turned out that what they wanted was for their names to be more easily distinguished from one another. Once they told me the issue, the solution (lowercase italic for the *and*) was obvious (to me).

BOB WOODWARD AND CARL BERNSTEIN

BOB WOODWARD & CARL BERNSTEIN

BOB WOODWARD AND CARL BERNSTEIN

BOB WOODWARD *and* CARL BERNSTEIN

It's confusing, on the design side, to be given direction without context. It's hard to reach a goal you can't see. There are a thousand ways to resolve any design question and the art director and designer are best equipped to think them through. Not: "Make it orange." But: "Can it be brighter?"

Nitpicking can ruin your cover. If you adhere to the advice so far, this won't be your problem, but it's worth repeating since it's endemic in design critique (from all corners). A cover design is an integrated idea, not an à la carte menu. Each piece relies on every other piece like a Rube Goldberg contraption. If the chute is moved, the ball won't make it into the maze, and then the weight won't fall on the scale making the toaster pop. Or a change to the title font (or size or color) may make every element around it shift its size and placement and color as well. Design direction coming from nondesigners, no matter how well intentioned, almost never understands how thought-through every detail on a cover already is. Pick enough nits and what was a strong or balanced or successful design is now a weaker and mushier one.

Talk to your agent. Many authors share the cover concepts they receive with a close circle of friends or family. This crowdsourcing of feedback may give you some perspective or fresh takes, or it may just muddy your thinking. Most people don't know how to respond to design and are just saying things because you've asked them to. If it's an option, your agent is the perfect person to talk it through with—someone squarely in your camp who understands the material and the landscape. An agent can help you prioritize and organize your thoughts and understands what changes are worth fighting for.

Some suggestions by the author are quick fixes and others will take a new cycle of thinking and designing. One round of this is appropriate and expected. More than that, and authors start depleting their supply of goodwill.

More Feedback

Once the author and in-house team have landed on a cover they all love (or at least one they've agreed on), it will be shared with the sales team, distributor, parent company, and key buyers, like those at Barnes & Noble or Walmart. Typically, the response is a thumbs up, but sometimes concerns are raised. These are the folks most in tune with what's happening in the current market and they can be biased toward already successful approaches. Outside-the-box designs can get pushback. But feedback from the people buying the books or selling them into bookstores is potent, and publishers will often make changes, even significant changes, based on their comments. (Very) occasionally, the folks in-house and the author will believe so strongly in the strength of a design that they will stand behind it despite a lukewarm response from the sales force.

The Final Cover

Some covers glide through. Other times, it's a struggle every step of the way. Many hoops are jumped through before a cover gets approved, and commercial, or other, issues can trump aesthetic ones. "Design by committee" is shorthand for a design that's diminished by too many voices pulling too many different directions. Sadly, that's the way things go (or are structured) at some publishing houses—designers lose authority over their work, which is chipped away until something that looked cool doesn't anymore (this can happen with the design of interiors too). Designer Peter Mendelsund describes this as "ugli-fication . . . in which designers—by request or demand—make their work uglier, one detail at a time (Can you change the font?; I don't like red; Can you use a different picture . . . ?)."[3] Sometimes everyone but the designer will huddle to critique and discuss a cover and compile a list of changes—which may make no design sense. Problem-solving *with* designers will be more fruitful than making visual or editorial demands in a vacuum. It's not that it hurts our feelings to be left out of the conversation (well, maybe a little)—organizations where art direc-tors' and designers' voices are valued, and are part of final decision-making, will end up with better-looking books.

Once cover design is approved, it's usually revealed, to larger or smaller fanfare, on social media and, eventually, on Amazon and other bookselling sites. It will also go into the publisher's catalog, which is used to sell to bookstores. Meanwhile, the manuscript is finished and copyedited, the interior of the book is designed, back-cover copy is written, blurbs are begged, and the marketing and PR machines roar to life. Just a few weeks before the cover is due to print, the full cover—back, spine, flaps—will be designed. Authors are usually shown the designed jacket or full cover, but any changes here are expected to be editorial (regarding sales copy or blurbs) rather than visual.

From Manuscript to Layout

Manuscripts are passed from writer to editor, editor to copyeditor, and copyeditor to designer (depending on the press, there may be some interstitial steps in there). The hand-off from editorial to design is called the design transmittal. This is when all the pieces for the inside of the book—final text, any art and captions, tables, or diagrams—are given to the designer. Once I have those materials in hand, I will pour the text into my design file. This is the moment where life as a manu-script ends and the journey as a book begins.

Markup

Designers expect to receive a manuscript that is sparkling clean and competently tagged. Markup (also called tagging, coding, or styling) is a labeling system in which each piece of text is classified by its function. Chapter titles are labeled chapter titles, running text is labeled as such. Different publishers use different sets of tags and different processes for encoding them. For a freelancer who works with many clients, switching between projects on a busy day can be like speaking a half dozen different languages.[4]

The parts of a manuscript may seem obvious and intuitive—in many cases they are—but in a more complex (usually nonfiction) book a designer might be juggling a hundred or more tags that reflect an intricate hierarchy and many varieties of text. Am I looking at two H2s or an H2 and an H3? Is this a bulleted list or a numbered one? I can't tell where an excerpt ends and the running text takes back up. The visual hierarchy and extra hard returns that authors use to make this clear are often only clear to them.

Tagging may seem a bit of administrative busywork, but it's as important to the clarity of text as where the commas go. (The task of tagging is often the responsibility of copyeditors, who are also checking all

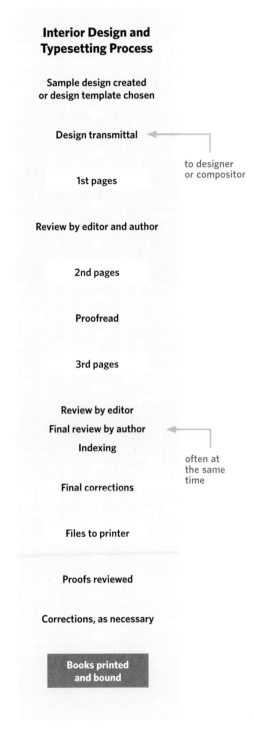

Interior Design and Typesetting Process

Sample design created or design template chosen

Design transmittal

to designer or compositor

1st pages

Review by editor and author

2nd pages

Proofread

3rd pages

Review by editor

Final review by author

Indexing

often at the same time

Final corrections

Files to printer

Proofs reviewed

Corrections, as necessary

Books printed and bound

Tagging Text

Text from the author looks like this. What is what?

> Summer Pies
> If you wish to make an apple pie from scratch, you must first invent the universe. —Carl Sagan
> Sweet
> Sweet pies are what everyone wants. There are so many ways to go. Cream pies and silk pies are special and luscious, but you can't beat old-fashioned, toss-in-some-fruit-and-sugar pies.
> Cherry
> Cherry pie is bright, tart, and feels like summer. But you do have to pit the cherries if you are using fresh.

The editor or copyeditor adds tags—visually (as shown here) or through Word Styles or XML. Now the structure is clear.

> \<h1\>Summer Pies
> \<pq\>If you wish to make an apple pie from scratch, you must first invent the universe. \<pqa\>—Carl Sagan\</pqa\>
> \<h2\>Sweet
> \<p\>Sweet pies are what everyone wants. There are so many ways to go. Cream pies and silk pies are special and luscious, but you can't beat old-fashioned, toss-in-some-fruit-and-sugar pies.
> \<h3\>Cherry
> \<p\>Cherry pie is bright, tart, and feels like summer. But you do have to pit the cherries if you are using fresh.

A designer who understands the structure can invent a suitable design.

Summer Pies

> *If you wish to make an apple pie from scratch,*
> *you must first invent the universe.* —CARL SAGAN

SWEET

Sweet pies are what everyone wants. There are so many ways to go. Cream pies and silk pies are special and luscious, but you can't beat old-fashioned, toss-in-some-fruit-and-sugar pies.

Cherry. Cherry pie is bright, tart, and feels like summer. But you do have to pit the cherries if you are using fresh.

those commas.) As in the days when editors marked up a manuscript with a blue pencil, tagging is *the* mode of communication between editors and designers—the x-ray that reveals the skeleton. I look to the tags to understand the structure of a text, and the structure of a text guides the design of the book. (Correct markup is also essential for proper conversion to digital formats; see page 161). If an editor doesn't fully understand the manuscript, it will show up in sloppy or even incorrect tagging. (The designer knows!) Tags aren't design direction; they aren't about how things look. If authors or editors have specific *stylistic* ideas or requests, that requires a different kind of communication—in writing or on the phone.

Sample Design

Book interiors usually begin with a sample design phase in which the designer works with a representative portion of text to figure out the design scheme for the entire book. The primary elements are thought through: what fonts at what sizes, how the text block will look (line length, line spacing, margins), where the page numbers and running heads will go, how the chapter display is styled, how the TOC is styled. Many publishing houses have style guides that dictate some aspects of this skeleton as well as typesetting variables like em dashes, fractions, hyphenation, and widows and orphans. Publishers who put out lots of books of straight, narrative text might create (or, I suppose, buy) interior design templates. That is, they can make a sample design, or a few sample designs, and use it for books with similar content. For instance, all their mysteries might be the same trim size, using the same fonts, margins, leading, etc. A design template is really only a sample design that is deployed over and over again. But even when using templates, designers or compositors must make decisions based on the material they're given. If the template's style works well for short chapter titles and the given book has long ones, they will need to adjust accordingly.

Illustrated and design-forward books have more variables, and more flexible page design, and need a lot of attention in this early stage (see chapter 5)—we will not be using a template here. For illustrated and other books with complex design issues (including poetry), authors will be part of the review and revision process for sample design. Whether authors see sample design for books of straight text will vary from publisher to publisher. If this is something that's important to you, ask.

The only definitive way to have a feel for the size of type and other elements, and the size of the page itself, is to see them printed out. I always, always, always make physical printouts (at 100 percent size and trimmed to crop marks) of a portion of my design so I can see how it actually looks. You don't need every page in print, but it's important to see each element. Editors and authors, if they're reviewing sample design, should do the same. The size on screen is often misleading.

Once typography and layout are agreed on, the designer will do a castoff, an estimate of the overall page count based on the proposed design. (Some publishing houses will give designers a target word-per-page goal to hit.) If the castoff doesn't align with expectations—the book was spec'd at 360 pages and the castoff has it at 460, before the index—this is the moment to adjust. That could mean revising the spec or revising the design, or both.

Full Layout

There are usually three rounds of layouts (could be more with an illustrated or particularly complex book) with reviews and proofreading by various players between each (see the chart on page 179). These days designed pages are usually sent around as PDFs and corrected, revised, and commented on—by the author, editor, and proofreader—digitally.

First pages, page proofs, first layout, first galleys, and *firsts* are all terms used to refer to the first complete set of designed pages. The types of corrections, and number of corrections, from authors and editors varies widely. I have some publishing clients who work hard to get the final manuscript close to perfect, and the only corrections coming back from first pages are typesetting ones. Other editors (or authors) use first pages as an editing round, and changes can be more extensive (groan). For visual books, first pages are a chance to note anything that is amiss or not flowing as intended. In those books, it is common to shift elements around, cut text to fit, and swap out images during the review of first pages. By second pages these issues should be (mostly) resolved and the focus will turn to proofreading and catching errors.

Depending on the level of changes made in the first round, a second round may need to go back to the editor and author for another look. If not, the layout is ready for proofreading. In most nonfiction books, an index will need to be compiled after the file has been proofed (sometimes indexing happens at the same time as proofreading, a situation that always makes me a little nervous). Designers (or compositors) input proofreading changes, style the index, and create a round asking for "final corrections." No editorial changes should be occurring at this point. It's all "add a period to the last paragraph on the copyright page"–level corrections. Editors can be stingy with authors as the final round nears. They worry that authors can't stop revising, and some can't. Other authors feel relieved to be finally finished reviewing and rereading their text.

After final checks, the file is prepped for, and sent to, the printer. Preparing files well is the mark of an experienced designer, work that is invisible to everyone on the editorial side. For illustrated books, it can be a complicated and time-consuming task.

Dummies and Proofs

Aside from my most creative thinking time—in the shower, of course—almost all of my designing occurs at the computer. Working on a book looks like gliding words and images across an illuminated plane. Spreads appear in a single two-dimensional box—the left-hand and right-hand pages separated not by a binding but by a single black line. This is how editors and authors and marketing folks see the book-in-progress as well. As the layout moves from design to review to corrections to final proofing stages, everyone experiences it in a flat, electronic form.

Obviously, that's not what printed books are actually like. They're made of paper and ink, not pixels and light. The paper isn't 100 percent white but has color, texture, weight, and feel. The binding can be tight or loose, eating up more or less of the page. Rather than the brilliant color you can achieve on the screen, a book makes its color through the application of ink into or onto paper that can be darker and duller. Getting a sense of the physical nature of the book, before it's printed, bound, and shipped to the store, is an important part of creating something beautiful and intentional.

A "dummy" is a version of a book with no printing in it. Although the pages and cover are blank, it's a representation of the dimensions, weight, and feel of the final form of the book. The paper, the length, the binding, the jacket (if there is one) are available to inspect and approve (or change, if necessary). Text-driven books in standard sizes and formats don't require dummies, but illustrated and other design-forward books often do. Authors are usually not privy to dummies, but editors, art directors, and designers review them to make sure the book they're envisioning is, in fact, the book they're going to get.

Printer's proofs come in two forms. The most common are called bluelines (or, often, Ozalids when printing outside of the United States) and show, at low quality, the position of all text and images. Publishers use these as a final visual proofreading of text, sequence, and placement. Many printers now use PDF proofs (sometimes referred to as e-blues or soft proofs) instead of printed pages. In my experience, authors rarely see or review these proofs.

Color proofs are always hard copies. The point of them is to show how color will appear in the final printed book, and they must be printed to do that. Color is tricky in printing—it is highly affected by the paper, ink, and the way image files have been set up (see page 148). For books in which color reproduction is important—which is most any book with color imagery—a color proofing round (and sometimes multiple rounds) is part of the production process and must be built into the schedule.[5]

Once proofs are approved, there's nothing left to do but wait for finished books. In some cases, printers send printed-but-not-bound jackets, covers, and full sets of pages—called F&Gs for *folded and gathered signatures*—for review before binding. Needing to make a change to an already printed book is traumatic and expensive. But less traumatic and expensive than making a change to an already printed and bound book.

Advances (as in royalty advances) are what publishers pay authors before they've sold any books. But it's also what we call the first, precious set of books that are shipped (by air) to the publisher in advance of the full bulk shipment that needs to travel by truck across the country or boat across the ocean. Advance copies of a book are stingily meted out. Often only a single copy goes to the author. But still, holding that first finished copy is cause for celebration, relief, and even awe, as well as a proud selfie on social media.

Self-Publishing

The development of ebooks, print-on-demand technology, desktop publishing software, and the robust marketplaces for books online has made it possible for anyone to publish a book. While some authors self-publish because they cannot find a foothold in the traditional system, others opt for it right off the bat because they want the control, and higher royalty rates, that self-publishing offers.

If you're self-publishing, you're up against the same challenge as every other author: how to get anyone outside family and friends to read your book (or even know that it exists). Without the guidance and support of a publishing house, you have to figure out everything yourself: editing, proofreading, platforms, formats, publicity, discoverability, and design. The most successful independent authors assemble a support team of professionals to help them in the areas where they can't, or don't want to, help themselves. These authors also understand the power of a strong visual identity for their website, social media, and—the anchor—book covers. For almost all, this requires hiring professional designers to help them.

Choosing a Designer

There are a lot of designers in the world with varying skills, expertise, and price. Some work on websites, some logos, some book covers, some interiors. The first step is to hire the appropriate designer for the task. Book design is a niche field; look for a designer who knows it well. We're discoverable through professional associations, self-publishing service providers, and "we're really cheap"–style websites. Some publishing services keep aggregated lists of designers and design resources (see page 213 for some specific direction here). When deciding whom to hire, consider the following.

Freelance Designer or Service Provider

If you have the budget, working one-on-one with a designer will give you the most control and opportunity for collaboration. If you plan to write a lot of books, in a series or not—or if you have written a lot of books and are ready to rebrand them—visual continuity will be facilitated by working with a single designer over a number of titles. There are also publishing services companies that offer a menu of design options, as well as other services, directed at the self-publishing author. This saves you the work of finding and vetting someone on your own and, ideally, ensures some structure around the process. You can also browse sites that host creative freelancers, sometimes for budget prices. You might find someone great here. But beware, these sites can be a rat's nest of misrepresentation, soulless and generic work, and poor communication.

Visual Style

Of course. Look at designers' portfolios, either on their personal website or on freelancer sites. Find someone whose covers you admire and who is working within your genre.

Experience

Do they have five or fifty examples of their work? Green designers can, of course, have great ideas, but you don't need two newbies rowing the canoe. If their portfolio is small, you might check that the covers are from actual published books and not student work or design practice. An experienced designer will have a deeper knowledge of genres and categories and will be able to guide you, and the process, more successfully. (They may also have clearer boundaries, for better or worse.)

Price

Prices vary (maybe widely) and quality will usually correspond. A higher design fee will buy experience and attention. Only you know how much you have to spend, but keep in mind this truism: fast, cheap, good—pick two.

Communication

Respectful, responsive communication is an important part of any working relationship (and any relationship at all, for that matter). I only want to work with people who get back to me in a timely manner, answer with complete information, meet agreed deadlines, manage expectations, and are generally pleasant. If the person you are feeling out as a designer fails at any of these, even in the first email, look elsewhere. The process is complicated enough without that added frustration.

See the appendix for a discussion of suggested terms between an author and designer and a sample freelance design contract.

Cover Design

While I don't think you should be your own cover designer, self-publishing does require you to be your own art director. Without the structure of a publishing house, it's up to the author to create the circumstances that will lead to an effective process and a successful design. Working with an experienced designer will make this job easier. If you're working one-on-one with a designer, you'll want to hand them a cover brief and have a conversation to discuss it. A publishing services provider will most likely ask you a prescribed series of questions, many of which echo the information in the brief. Because you're the only person that the design needs to satisfy, the rounds of feedback and iteration will be simpler than the tangle of approvals necessary through a traditional publisher. Here are my suggestions for an effective process.

The Brief

No matter what situation you've decided on for your cover design, write a creative brief. The brief helps *you* clarify what it is you want, which, in turn, will increase the chances that someone can give it to you. Return to page 66 to see the elements that belong in a cover brief.

Comps

A critical piece of the cover brief is the competitive (or comparable) research. The best way to study the other books in your genre (what will be sitting on the bookshelf, or browser screen, with yours) is to paste thumbnails of bestselling or relevant covers into a single document. There is nothing like seeing these covers, lined up together at thumbnail size, to elucidate their common traits: type style, color, kind of imagery, composition, and level of design polish. It will help you think about what you do and don't want for your cover. If you've picked the right designer for your project, they may know more about this than you. If your book is hard sci-fi, look for designers who have demonstrated depth in that area. They'll understand the conventions of the genre. If your book is memoir, same.

Imagery

Do you want photography or illustration (or neither) on your cover? Where are those images going to come from? Although you can imagine anything in the world, you may not be able to lay your hands on a suitable image. If you want original art for your cover, you may need an illustrator. (See the resources section for places to source imagery.) Full-service design sites will offer stock imagery, usually as part of the package. If you're working one-on-one with a freelancer, the cost of images will be in addition to the design fee. And if you're planning on providing or finding the imagery yourself, talk to the designer about it first. Some art doesn't translate successfully for covers because it's too busy, too literal, or leaves no space for type. All imagery in a book—and especially on the cover—must be high resolution and high quality.

Self-Publishing Design Process

Front Cover	Interior	Full Cover
Find a designer	Sample design	Cover template or spine width from printer
Write creative brief	Design transmittal	
Discuss	1st pages	Back cover copy, including blurbs, author bio, any other elements
		Barcode
1st round covers	Review by author	Full cover design
Feedback	2nd pages	Review by author
Revision		
2nd round covers	Review by author	**Cover file for printer**
Refining	Proofread	
Final front cover	3rd pages	
	Indexing (if needed)	
	Final review	
	Final files for print and/or ebook	

Type

It's helpful to point to type styles or fonts that you like and think would be appropriate for your cover. The designer should be familiar with what you're pointing out and will have insight into what will or won't be successful in this context.

Series and Brand

It's no secret that the secret to successful self-publishing is writing a lot, often in series. If that's your plan, communicate that to the designer. Creating a design for a one-off is a different project than creating a design that will be iterated in a series. (Creating a series look may also be more expensive than designing for a single title.) Even if you're not planning on writing in series, tying your books together through some aspect of visual branding can be a good way for your future devoted readers to recognize your work.

Feedback

Here's a place where the costs and benefits of not working with a publishing house are made clear. On the bright side, there's only one person to please, and it's you! On the other side, it's up to you, and only you, to evaluate and respond effectively, to shepherd the not-quite-right first round toward the "chef's kiss" final cover. This can be a challenge, particularly if design isn't your first language. An experienced art director might say, "The palette feels too quiet, can you make it pop more?" while you might say, "Boy, I hate that green, use purple instead." You both may be responding to the same problem—the colors should be bolder—but the art director understands the issue (and speaks the language) while you only know that something is wrong with the colors. A traditionally published author is seeing covers that have been vetted by an experienced in-house team. Your cover is up to you.

You'll probably be presented with three different cover ideas (or however many has been agreed on). Once you see them, it may be quite clear which direction is the strongest and which should be abandoned. Seeing *something* is so different from only imagining.

Use the comps. If you don't know how to evaluate the designs, or even if you do, go back to the group of thumbnail comps you so thoughtfully gathered earlier and pop in your cover options. Comparing them to their companions, and competitors, will help you see them as book covers within the context of other book covers. Which ones draw your eye? Which describe your book best? Which sit within the genre most comfortably? Do any feel *too* similar to other already-published books?

Write, then talk. The most useful way to relay feedback is to write it up and then talk it out. Writing out your thoughts forces you to clarify them and will give the designer a chance to absorb and consider them. But we all know what back-and-forth on email can be like. These are complex and subtle questions and worth a voice-to-voice exchange. A phone or video conversation will cover more ground, provide more context, and tend to engender trust and goodwill on both sides.

Start with why. If there are aspects you think you don't like or may want changed, start by asking the designer why they made the choices they did. While you may wonder about another typeface for the title, there will be a host of reasons the designer picked this one. They'll tell you if you ask: "It's narrow and fits the space." "It's wide and takes up less horizontal space (so more room for the image)." "It's sans serif and therefore less busy." "It's bold and reads well against the background." "I wanted the cover to feel Gothic/modern/historic." Now that you know, give those ideas a chance to move you forward constructively or change your perspective.

Focus on impact. Just because the designer has a reason for every choice they made doesn't mean you have to like them all. Focus on overall impact and what you'd like to see further developed or rerouted. "Make it beachier!" "I'd like to see more of the heroine and less of the manor house." "How can the title stand out more?" Or even, "Can it be more like this (other) cover?" If you have the benefit of a phone conversation, talk together, broadly, about how to accomplish those goals. But know that the details will be worked out in the designing and should not be overdetermined or micromanaged. I can't say it enough times: leave the designing to the designers.

Be open. You took on the expense of hiring a professional designer for your cover. Let them bring their expertise to it. An art director doesn't evaluate a design based on their personal preferences but on what they think is effective. You may not be a fan of red, but it might be just the right thing for this cover. Be open to the ideas the designer brings to the project and listen when they explain the logic behind their choices.

Reassess? If the first round of covers feel really off-key to you, go back to the brief. Talk through how the covers do or do not respond to genre, audience, and the original design direction. Strategize with the designer on how to right the ship. It may make sense for the next round to be quick and sketchy to be sure you are in sync before spending too much more time and effort. If the designer's ideas aren't headed in a direction you would have imagined, or like, it's possible you're a bad aesthetic match. You might consider whether it's worth it to cut ties early, pay the kill fee, and find someone else.

Stop. Your agreement with the designer should specify the number of rounds of cover design, although some service providers offer unlimited rounds until you are satisfied (sounds like a trip through hell to me). Regardless, if you find yourself at round four or five and are still asking for changes, do yourself a favor and stop. You're probably picking your cover to death. (See page 176.)

The Rest of the Cover

Front cover design is always first. If your book will be published as ebook only, that's as far as you need to go. Physical books need a spine and back cover too (jacketed books also need flaps). Full covers—back, spine, front—are created from sizing templates provided by whoever is doing the printing. To get the spine width, the printer will need to know how many pages the book has, and what paper you've chosen.

That means *you* will need to know this information, and you can't know it until you have the final (or close-to-final) interior layout. Once you do, you should provide the spine width (or cover template) along with all the back-cover elements to the designer: the description of the book, blurbs if you've got them, author bio and photo, the barcode, shelving category, publishing and printing info, and art and design credits (the designer may be able to provide these). See page 94 for the aspects of spine and back-cover design.

Interior Design

For the best-looking, smoothest-reading, most authoritative, polished book, I recommend a professional designer for your interior. If you've read the earlier parts of this book, you know how much thought and skill goes into high-quality page design. Chances are you aren't going to learn to do this well on YouTube in the next month. If you decide to pay for interior layout, find someone who does that for a living. Many design generalists will not be familiar with the particular conventions of book design. If your book has a complex hierarchy or is visually focused (that includes children's books), you will most certainly need a professional to manage this complex task and make it beautiful. Okay, that's the pitch. Here's your part.

The Manuscript

Authors should deliver a complete manuscript including all the pieces of text in a single document. Chapters, front matter, and back matter should not be separated into individual files. If there will be images in the book, all final, high-resolution images should also be delivered in your design transmittal (as separate files, not embedded in your Word doc). If you're still writing, editing, or gathering your images, it's not yet time for interior design.

The best thing you can do for the designer is present a professionally copyedited, clean, and marked-up manuscript. I don't expect individual authors to master XML markup, but it's within everyone's capacity to review their manuscript for stylistic consistency and clean up the most obvious typographic litter (extra spaces, returns, and tabs). Levels of hierarchy should be made clear in some fashion—preferably through the use of styles in your writing program or, less ideally, bracketed tags [bulleted list], [end of bulleted list], etc. Don't make the designer guess what's an A-head and what's a B-head.

Art

If the book includes art, it should be high quality and high resolution. Image resolution is sometimes overlooked because images, even low-resolution images, can look perfectly good on a screen. But screens and printed pages require different levels of fidelity to look good, and screen appearance isn't a reliable indicator. Images *must* be at print-quality resolution (commonly called high resolution or high res) for acceptable results when printed. (The magic number for print resolution is 300 dpi [dots per inch] at 100 percent size.) Of course, any and all art used should be properly licensed and paid for.

Files should be well organized and well named. The best system for naming images is to number them in the order they will appear in the book and include a short descriptive title so that the designer can confirm they're placing the right image in the right spot (001_ducks, 002_Donald, 003_Orlando). Images that aren't taken by professionals often need Photoshop work—to adjust contrast and tone, convert to grayscale, and do general cleanup. Discuss whose responsibility this is. Photoshop work is slow and meticulous. If this will be a necessary part of the designer's job, that should be factored into the design fee.

Sample Design

Sample design is always an important step, and it's critical for self-publishers working with a new designer. The sample design process will ensure that you and the designer are in agreement on the treatment of all elements before layout begins, cutting down on confusion later. Designers should be well versed in text fonts for both print and ebooks. Follow their lead. See page 181 for more on sample design.

Review and Proofreading

A book will need at least two rounds of proofing before it goes to press. The first will be a review by the author to make sure every page has been laid out correctly and the text is exactly as you want it. All text corrections and comments should be made right on the pages of the PDF for the most accurate communication. Under no circumstance should you make changes for the designer within your original manuscript. This would require the designer to reflow the text and trigger (huge!) additional fees. (Yes, I'm trying to scare you.)

Once your changes are input and you've reviewed and approved the layout, there's another crucial round: proofreading. A final review by you, your partner, or your mother isn't sufficient. Having entered proofreaders' changes for twenty years, I'm here to champion their professional eyes and the work they do to purge errors, ensure informational correctness, stylistic consistency, and wipe that final dust cloth over the text to make it shine. To my mind, this isn't optional.

Hiring, managing, and paying a proofreader is the responsibility of the author. You should ask the designer for any instructions for the proofreader or put them in direct contact so that the proofreader marks changes in the best way for the designer (who's going to input them). If the proofreader's corrections have editorial consequences, the author should be consulted before those changes are made.

I always give authors a final review after proofreading changes have been input. Designers are human and sometimes mistakes get introduced in the process of making corrections (this is an argument for keeping correction rounds to a minimum). The final review isn't an opportunity to continue making changes; only errors should be corrected from now on. Once the author gives the thumbs up, a print-ready file (usually a PDF) will be created.

DIY Formatting

People can reasonably disagree on the importance of professional design for (simple) book interiors. For authors who are writing fiction or memoir or other text-only books with a straightforward structure and are on a tight budget, DIY formatting may be sufficient. To my eyes, there are many (many) tells that a layout wasn't created by a professional and even a typical reader may be distracted by occasional weird formatting choices and inconsistencies. This may be a tradeoff you can live with.

One of the clear benefits of formatting your own interior is the ability to make changes as they come up. A great perk of ebook and POD technology is the ease in which a book can be revised, even after it's published. If you're the master of your interior layout, you can make corrections, update links and resources, or even decide to change the ending at will.

But anyone who tells you that formatting a book is easy—and many service providers targeting self-publishing authors do—is out to sell you something. Turning a text file into a PDF or EPUB file might not be that complicated (it's not that *not* complicated, though) but creating a clear and consistent, not to mention elegant, layout across hundreds of pages and thousands of words isn't an easy task for anyone. If you decide to take it on, here are some principles to keep in mind.

Use Good Tools

Use writing tools for writing and layout tools for layout. Word processing software and dedicated writing tools are great for crafting a story and just abysmal at design, layout, and formatting. Trying to wrangle a clear, consistent book out of them is an exercise in frustration and usually a failed one. In my experience, formatting templates that are sold to be used inside of Word or Pages are complicated and snaggy. You have to be a designer already to use them well. Uploading text documents to service providers that convert them for you is simply crossing your fingers and hoping for the best.

Adobe InDesign is the professional tool that book designers use and the best software for professional layout. But it's also a costly and multifaceted program that may be more than you need. Streamlined programs designed specifically for laying out book interiors exist and are the best option for nondesigners. Part of their key to success is that they limit the options available, forcing authors to choose from a menu of mostly already good choices (this isn't the case for programs like Word, which offer many bad choices). They're also set up to deal with complex layout issues like aligning text columns across spreads and dealing with widows and orphans. See the resources section for some ideas.

Remember That Print and Ebooks Are Different

Professional designers think differently about the design of print and ebooks and so should you. Print books are WYSIWYG. What you've laid on that page will appear just as you see it in your print-ready PDF and, barring printing mishaps, the way it will look in the finished book. Ebooks don't behave as obediently. Create one file for your print book and another for the ebook version. These are some of the differences.

For ebooks:

- Remove all but the most essential images and anchor them to text.
- Set body text left aligned.
- Turn hyphenation off.
- Check (twice) that hyperlinks are live and current.
- Remove running heads (or feet) and page numbers.

For print books:

- Place images thoughtfully.
- Set body text fully justified.
- Use sensible hyphenation settings (see page 204).
- Remove underlining and color from hyperlinks (*all* versions of your book should avoid long URLs and use short names for websites instead).
- Review the layout in spreads, making sure facing pages align (for narrative text) and minimizing widows, orphans, and runt lines.

Avoid the Worst Mistakes

It takes years of experience to become fluent at typography and text design. But dedicated layout programs have come a long way in solving for the most irksome typographic distractions—preventing widows and orphans, balancing pages, and preventing short pages. They set generous margins and put space above your headers and below your chapter titles. They will save you from most of your worst impulses. In addition, you can improve the look of your books with the following best practices.

- Read through the Type Etiquette section of this book (page 204).
- Keep elements consistent. This is one of the most common errors in DIY layouts and is more of a mechanical issue than an aesthetic one. Review *every page* closely to make sure spacing and styling is applied correctly and consistently to every single piece of text in the book.
- Turn off hyphenation for titles and all other headings.
- Set short passages of text, including captions, lists, and pull quotes, left aligned.
- Centered text requires a lot of care. If you're not up for adjusting every instance, default to left alignment, which is more forgiving, for all elements, including titles.
- Include sensible running heads (for print).
- Don't include running heads on pages with chapter titles.
- Keep type off images.
- Wrapping text around images requires a lot of care. If you're not up for adjusting every instance to avoid big gaps, strange breaks, or tight lines, avoid this maneuver.
- Keep emphasis quiet: don't abuse bold or all caps and avoid underlining altogether.
- The only place a drop cap is appropriate is at the start of a chapter. No. Where. Else.
- Avoid drop shadows and other "fancy" effects on type and images.
- Have a professional proofread before publishing.
- Do a design and consistency proof of all versions of your book in all formats before publishing (for ebooks, proof on multiple devices and platforms).
- Remember: the goal of book design is clarity, not decoration. Your readers are here for your words and ideas; give them to them in the most direct way you can.

The Finished Book

Publishing is full of big moments. For authors: landing an agent, finishing a manuscript and selling it to a publisher, or deciding to realize a project on their own terms. For editors and agents: reading something that excites them, winning a project, bringing it to the world in its best form. The biggest moment of all (perhaps aside from making the *New York Times* bestseller list) is holding that first printed copy in your hands—the uncracked spine, the inky smell, the pages sticky with newness. Authors have been known to stroke their book's cover, clutch it to their chest, shriek with joy, and gaze down at it with love eyes. All the work made material.

But a book isn't really for its author, or editor, or designer, or anyone at the publishing house. We make books for readers. People write for many reasons, but publishing seeks an audience. Readers might spend days or weeks (or months or years) with a book. Their fingers touch each page. Their eyes pass over every word. Their minds absorb the ideas, language, and images. A book is a meeting place for writers and readers. Cover art, typography, space, rhythm, balance, color—design!—are the doors through which they enter.

Postscript

I set out to write this book because I felt that the authors and editors I work with didn't know enough about book design, and there seemed to be nowhere for them to go to figure it out. Books about design are for designers. The websites that try to explain book design are often piecemeal and confusing, describing the *what* but not the *why*. I wanted those on the editorial side to understand design words and moves but also the logic of design—not for the fun of it (although it is fun) but so that we can have better conversations, better experiences, better books.

I hope this book has given you some insight into how type works and why line length matters. I hope you have a deeper feel for the styling of headings and how the words of a title impact cover design. Most of all, I hope it helps you *see* design, and what it brings to the table, more clearly.

This book is an argument for the value of design, and also for the voice and ideas of the designer. Publishing is a long process and design often comes late in the game. Too often there's a disconnect between what I'm given to work with and what I'm asked to do with it. I encourage you to consider how your book will ultimately perform on the page while you're still writing and developing it. Bring a designer in— early. Allow us to engage editorially with you, and the work, while the important choices are still being made. Effective design is entwined with content. If you try to smooth it on once the cake is already baked, you've missed the point.

You learn things when you read books, and you learn things when you write them too. Researching and writing this book, I discovered a lot about design (and myself), including that there were things I felt strongly about only because I had believed them for a long time. I appreciated the opportunity to question my own preconceptions and habits after twenty years of designing books and find that some no longer serve. Some may have always been unfounded. Examining our old patterns—in design, in writing, in life!—opens us to new ideas and creative paths. Turns out, sometimes there *is* a reason to use bold italic.

Appendix

Type Etiquette

Typesetting isn't the same as typing and there are a handful of small, but apparent, pro moves that are as common to book designers as salt to the chef. Many of them fall within the gray area between editorial and typographic concerns. If you are formatting your own interior layout, or just want a really spiffy manuscript that your editor will love you for, note the following.

Capitalization

Many writers and editors set their titles and headings in all caps as a way of creating hierarchy within their Word doc. And sometimes designers choose to style titles and headings in all caps in a final typeset layout. But sometimes we don't. It's surprisingly hard to reverse engineer from all caps to title case (also called headline style, see the glossary), which requires decision-making about which words are capped and which are not. (Shifting from title case to all caps, on the other hand, is a breeze.) Please note: all caps is a type styling decision in the same mode as choosing size or boldness for distinctive pieces of text. In a manuscript, all titles and headings should always be set in title case. The designer will make the call of how to style them from there.

The Hyphen and Dashes

The hyphen and dashes commonly used in typography are often confused with each other. These are three different characters with three different uses.

- The **hyphen** is the shortest of the three and it joins words together. I've whiled away many pleasant hours with *The Chicago Manual of Style* (*CMOS*) hyphenation guide (*CMOS*, 17th ed., section 7.89) which advises on the appropriate use of hyphenation for editorial style. The hyphen also does god's work at the end of lines; see facing page.

- The **en dash** is the middle sister, longer than the hyphen, shorter than the em dash. The en dash expresses range: "Virginia Woolf (1882–1941) is the mother of modernist literature."

Hyphen	▬
En dash	▬▬
Em dash	▬▬▬

- The **em dash** is the width of a capital *M* at whatever size and font you're using. The em dash keeps words or passages apart. "Shoot—another thing to remember."

Line Breaks / Hyphenation Settings

Many publishers have a house style for hyphenation settings at the end of lines. That is, these rules are fluid and different publishers make different choices. Making sense is the only *must*. Still, if I ruled the world, I would do it like this. (And I always break my own rules when necessary.)

- There should be minimum three letters before a hyphen, minimum three letters after a hyphen.
- Always hyphenate words at their syllable break (check the dictionary when unclear).
- Avoid hyphenating words that can possibly cause confusion as to their meaning when broken (*the-rapist* should be avoided[1]).
- Don't hyphenate proper nouns (this is the first rule I'll break, if needed, particularly with names that are used repeatedly in a manuscript).
- Don't hyphenate already-hyphenated compound words or phrases.
- Don't hyphenate words that are touching other dashes.
- Don't hyphenate the last word in a column or on a page.
- Don't hyphenate the last word of a paragraph.
- Don't hyphenate URLs, except if, and where, the hyphen is inherently part of the URL name (and in which case, break the line *before* the hyphen).

Ellipses

Space. Period. Space. Period. Space. Period. Space. Designers don't use the "tight" ellipsis character, which is simply too tight to make its point. If the ellipsis is meant to occur at the end of a full sentence, the sequence above starts after the final period of the sentence, resulting in four dots overall.

Numbers

- Fractions are always stacked.
- Percent and dollar signs should usually be spelled out.
- A sentence should begin with a word, not a numeral. "Two thousand twenty was not a good year." Or, even better, sentences should be written so they do not begin with a number: "The year 2020 was positively dreadful."
- In narrative text, the numbers one through one hundred should be spelled out, as should other round numbers over one hundred (although text that contains measurements often retains numerals).
- Whenever possible, numerals should be on the same line as their unit of measurement. This is confusing:
  Add then bake from 5 to 7
  minutes or until golden brown.

Quotation Marks and Primes

American quotation marks (and apostrophes) are called raised commas because they are raised commas. They should not be confused with the double prime (") or prime characters ('), which are straight ticks. Primes aren't a different style of quotation mark (or apostrophe) but different characters altogether with totally different functions, indicating feet (for a single) and inches (for a double) (they can also indicate minutes and seconds and other mathematical and scientific measures). There's nothing that screams sloppy design like the substitution of primes (or what writers might think of as "straight quotes") for actual quotes and apostrophes.

"hooray"   6'3"

Quotation marks   Prime and double prime marks

The American convention is double quote marks for dialogue and single quote marks for dialogue that appears within dialogue. In the UK, these conventions are reversed. Also, in books for American audiences, punctuation is generally kept inside quote marks, while in the UK, punctuation often sits outside the marks. Other countries use other typographic characters and methods for signaling dialogue.

Spaces and Tabs

Many manuscripts that come to me ready for design are lousy with extra spaces: at the end of a paragraph, at the beginning of a paragraph, to indicate a new paragraph, or to center or indent text. These wanton spaces wreak havoc—they must be removed (designers don't play with multiple spaces), and then it can be confusing what was the intended spacing. Let me put it to you plain: There is *never* a reason for two clicks on the space bar (much less eight or ten clicks). Never. Use the tab key for indentation and a single space at all other times. There are buttons on your word processor's tool bar to center text or indent an entire passage. If an extra long space is required (common for poetry, for instance), that should be notated within brackets and called out to the designer in a cover letter. Designers have lots of ways to create additional space on a line and it's never by double spacing.

Freelance Design Contract

When authors (or editors) are hiring freelance designers, terms must be stated in writing beforehand. This can be done in a formal contract or laid out more casually in an email, depending on each party's level of comfort. Most publishers will have their own contracts, but when working directly with authors, I address the following issues in my agreements.

Please note: this isn't a substitute for legal advice. All parties should consult a literary agent or attorney as needed. The Author's Guild (authorsguild.org) also has legal resources for authors.

Title and Specs

For a cover:
- format (paperback, hardcover, ebook, audiobook)
- trim size
- final set-in-stone title, subtitle, author name, and *all* text that belongs on the cover

For interiors:
- approximate word count
- full color, two-color, or only black
- number of images or illustrations (including tables and diagrams)

Design Rounds

My agreements are always specific about the number of initial cover designs (three is standard) and the number of expected design "rounds" (again, three is standard, with the third round being understood as a refining round—not a round of new ideas). I also stipulate that all images and fonts be legally licensed and that the author is expected to pay if art or fonts need to be purchased.

For interiors, I specify two rounds of sample design (here's my initial sample design, here's the revised sample design based on your feedback) and three rounds of the full layout (including a proofreading round). Full layout should not begin before the sample is approved and then will be based on that sample.

Changes

If there are *significant* changes to text or specs after design has begun, or changes to the design approach after sample design has been approved, it'll cost you. This is of course relative, but in my mind changes that will cause me more than fifteen minutes of redesign are significant. Think through your needs beforehand. Make approvals carefully. I usually charge an hourly rate for any work above and beyond what was originally agreed.

Timeline

Set realistic, comfortable deadlines for designs *and* responses. In professional production schedules, deadlines for design *and* for feedback and corrections are included. Design happens at the end of the process, and waiting for the designer can be excruciating for authors who are itching to publish. It also happens that designers send designs and wait inordinately for the author to respond. If the job is a rush, it should be charged that way.

Delivery

Designers should deliver a high-resolution or print-ready PDF for all print jobs and a verified EPUB for ebooks. Both print and ebooks need a separate file for the cover. It isn't the designer's job to upload files or participate in print proofing rounds unless you've agreed to that beforehand. Also consider how you will handle any corrections that are needed after the delivery of the files (this can be done with an hourly fee). If ownership of native files is important to you, include it in your terms. Native files are the original, revisable Photoshop, Illustrator, or InDesign files in which the design was created.

Payment

Payment is traditionally half upon "signing"—that is, upon agreement of the terms—and half upon final delivery. A "kill fee" is what the designer is paid if the job is canceled before completion. If a full first round of designs has been created, the signing payment (half the full amount) is an appropriate kill fee. If three full rounds have been worked through and either of the parties don't think a resolution is near, or feel the relationship has deteriorated beyond the point of usefulness, a payment of the full fee—if the designer has fulfilled their responsibilities—is appropriate.

Use

Most design work is work for hire so the author, or client, is the owner once it is complete. It is understood, however, that the designer/creator can use the work for self-promotion on their website, in their portfolio, and on social media. In my agreements, I specify that work in progress remains mine, as well as any rejected designs (maybe I'll use that idea somewhere else sometime).

Designers expect to be credited on the back cover, flap, or copyright page of your book.

If the design is so good that the author wants to create commercial merch around it—tote bags or coffee mugs or what have you—it is expected that they would kick back some percentage of those sales to the designer. Again, specific language in an agreement should address that if it's a possibility. (Alas, not usually the case.)

Here's a sample of a contract I might use.

DESIGN AGREEMENT

For the design of a book tentatively titled *The Design of Banjos* to be published by Squirrelly Press in 2024.

DESIGN FEE $6,000

Designer's Responsibilities: The designer will conceive of and execute the design for the cover and interior of the book, *The Design of Banjos*, the specifications of which are: 6 × 9-inch trim size, paperback, two-color interior with illustrations, approximately 240 pages in length.

Client's Responsibilities: The client is responsible for all editorial and administrative aspects of this project. The

client will ensure that art and text be delivered according
to the schedule and in an organized manner. Proofreading
and all other feedback and corrections will be collated and
managed by the client.

Design Process: The designer will provide sample design
pages showing examples of the major graphic elements of the
book. The designer understands that there may be requested
changes to the sample design, and the designer will not
begin execution of the interior of the book until the sample
design has been approved.

Once a design approach has been agreed upon, the book
will be executed accordingly. If *significant* changes in the
general design approach are requested after approval has been
made, work caused by those changes will be charged at $150
per hour. Additionally, if changes are made to the project
specifications after the design process begins that require
significant reworking of the established design approach, work
caused by those changes will be charged at $150 per hour.

Three rounds of interior pages, including a proofreading
round, are expected. At each phase, corrections will be
resolved between interested parties and collated into
a single document before being given to the designer.
Additional rounds will be charged at $150 per hour.

Three rounds of cover design are expected. Any and all
text (or other) elements required on the front cover of
the book must be provided prior to the first round of cover
design.

Payment: Payments shall be made $2,000 upon signing of this
agreement; $2,000 upon delivery of a full first layout; and
$2,000 upon the delivery of print-ready files to the client.
All invoices must be paid within thirty days of receipt.

The client will be responsible for all project expenses
including postage, copying, artwork, and fonts. No expenses
over $50 will be made without prior approval. All expenses
over $500 must be paid directly by the client.

The client will provide the designer with a complimentary
copy of the book upon publication.

Schedule: Design will be completed in accordance with a
production schedule to be mutually agreed upon. Missed or
late deadlines by artist, author, or publisher will require
respective shifting of deadlines by the designer. The
designer can guarantee the final mechanical date only if all
deadlines are met.

Proofing of final project: The designer shall make every effort to ensure the final publication is free of any grammatical, spelling, or stylistic errors, but it is agreed that (1) it is the client's ultimate responsibility to ensure that no such errors appear and (2) that the designer is not responsible or held liable for any errors that do appear in the final publication.

Permissions: All images that appear in the final publication have been provided by the client and/or legally licensed. The designer will not be liable for the improper use of any images. The client will hold harmless and indemnify the designer against any liability relating to copyright and usage in relation to this project.

Kill Fee: In the event of cancellation of the project after sample design has been submitted, a fee of $2,000 for work completed shall be paid by the client. Once the designer has executed a first galley design of the entire book, the full sum of the agreement is due regardless of postponement, cancellation, or other outcome of the publication of the book.

Ownership of Work: Until full payment has been made, the designer retains ownership of all original work or parts contained therein, whether preliminary or final.

Credit Line: A design credit shall appear on the copyright page of the book stating the following: Design by Debbie Berne.

Delivery: The designer will deliver the final files as InDesign CC files and/or high-resolution PDFs, as preferred by the printer.

By signing below both parties are agreeing to the fees and terms outlined above.

Resources

Below are some of my most trusty resources. I hope most of them will be around for many years to come. That said, things (and URLs) change. Dependable tools sometimes lose their magic and even better sites and software come to take their place. (There is little doubt that the widespread use of AI-generated art is going to shake up the stock image industry in the next decade). As of this printing, here's where to find . . .

A Professional Book Designer

Some designers focus on working with self-publishing authors and others stick primarily with traditional publishers. Some do both. Here are some ways to locate us:

- Look for our names (on the copyright page, back flap, or back cover) of books whose design you admire. Most designers will have a website or social media feed where you can see more of their work and reach out to them. Designers who work in-house for a publisher may, or may not, take on freelance work.
- Visit AIGA (aiga.org), the professional organization for designers, which includes searchable listings of their members.
- Browse the aggregated list of (partially vetted) freelance designers on websites like Reedsy (reedsy.com) and Joanna Penn (thecreativepenn.com).
- Check out the website ineedabookcover.com, which is a visual directory of cover design and cover designers.
- Hire a full-service provider for self-publishing authors. These services usually include design.
- Talk to the people who are editing or otherwise helping you with your book. Publishing professionals usually know other reliable publishing professionals. Word of mouth is a good way to find a designer.

Fonts

Fonts can be found—for fee or free—all over the internet. I stay away from free fonts (except through Google fonts), which are more likely to be glitchy, incomplete, or stolen from a legitimate source. You'll be in good hands with any of the sites below.

Creative Market. I go to creative market when I'm looking for something very of-the-moment. The strength is trendiness, not classics; display type, not body type (creativemarket.com).

Fonts in Use. You can't buy fonts on this site, but it's a great place to *look* at fonts (in use) and see what styles work well in what scenarios. It also provides information about fonts and links to sellers, when available (fontsinuse.com).

Google Fonts. There are fonts available for free download here with a focus on fonts appropriate for digital use and for use in many languages and alphabets (fonts.google.com).

MyFonts. This is a huge marketplace of traditional and contemporary fonts that can be licensed individually without a subscription (myfonts.com). (Be sure to read the license agreement.)

Stock Images

Searching for and selecting stock art is a skill in itself. Here are some of my regular haunts.

Alamy. This is an enormous library of stock photo and illustration (alamy.com).

Getty Images / Istockphoto. Images from Getty will have a higher price tag and tend to be higher quality. Getty is for photos. Illustration is limited and not their strong suit. Istockphoto is their discount sibling (with a more robust illustration selection) (gettyimages.com and istockphoto.com).

Noun Project. This is a resource for free icons and other one-color line art (nounproject.com).

Shutterstock. This is my go-to for stock illustration (less so for photos). You want generic? They've got generic. Millions of it (shutterstock.com).

Stocksy. I look here for reasonably priced, somewhat more interesting stock photography (stocksy.com).

Software and Tools

A tool is only as good as the person who wields it. Nondesigners usually don't make strong designs, even with strong tools. That said, if you are working on your own, Jane Friedman (janefriedman.com) and Joanna Penn (thecreativepenn.com) both offer solid advice on tools for cover design, interior formatting, and ebook conversion. Here's my shortlist.

Adobe Creative Suite. This is the tool professional designers use; it includes InDesign, Photoshop, and Illustrator (among other programs) and can be had with a monthly subscription. This isn't for the dabbler; it will take a serious effort to become comfortable with these tools (adobe.com).

Canva. This is an easy-to-navigate online tool for cover design (and many other design situations), and it includes a big library of fonts and stock images, layout templates, and the freedom to break away from templates (canva.com).

Vellum. Of the options I've seen for interior design for print and ebook conversion, Vellum is the easiest and most elegant (vellum.pub).

Inspiration

The very best way to get inspired by book design is to spend an afternoon at your local bookstore where you can actually *hold* and *look inside* books. But it's fun to browse the web too. The recommendations below focus on cover design, the most public part of book design.

The Academy of British Cover Design. British book covers look different from American book covers, in a good way! Browse the archives of their annual cover design competition, which includes genre categories like children's, YA, and mystery (abcoverd.co.uk).

AIGA Design Archives. Enjoy twenty years of winners from AIGA's highly-respected 50 Books | 50 Covers design competition. The 50 Books half includes consideration of the physical book and interior design (designarchives.aiga.org).

Book Cover Archive. This is no longer active, but it's still a great resource for contemporary cover design. Pull up that grid and be wowed (bookcoverarchive.com).

The Casual Optimist. This blog includes monthly selections of interesting cover design (heavily biased toward literary fiction) (casualoptimist.com).

Literary Hub. The site presents roundups of favorite cover designs (again, mostly focused on fiction) every month (lithub.com).

She Designs Books. This is an Instagram feed focusing on contemporary cover design by women (@shedesignsbooks).

Glossary

Publishing and book production have their own nomenclature, but it can be slippery. It's not unusual to talk with an art director, editor, printer, or other designer that names things differently than I do. Publishing houses, particularly, develop their own vocabulary for their processes, which may be confusing to outsiders. I've gathered what I consider the most common terminology below (and noted some places where alternatives are used). Don't be surprised if someone you're working with uses lingo other than what's described here. But you'll certainly be safe using the terms below.

alignment. The arrangement of lines of text, which can be **justified**, centered, or **ragged**.

alt text (alternative text). A description of an image in an ebook (or other digital media) that does not appear on the screen. Alt text is used to improve accessibility for vision-impaired readers as well as allowing the content of images to appear in searches.

ARC (advanced reader copy). Printed or digital versions of a book sent, usually to reviewers, booksellers, and other industry people, before the final version is complete.

back matter. The portion of a book that falls after the main body of a book. Can include acknowledgments, appendixes, resources, endnotes, bibliography, index, credits, information about the typeface, the author, other contributors, and the publisher. This glossary is part of the back matter of this book.

binding. The name for the covering of a book, e.g., **paperback, hardcover**. *Or* the manner in which the sheets of a book are attached to the covering, e.g., **perfect binding, case binding**.

BLAD (basic layout and design). A small, representative portion of a book, either printed or as a **PDF**, used for sales and marketing purposes.

bleed. To extend past the trimmed sheet of a page or cover. Art that extends past the page on all four sides is called a full bleed.

bluelines. A kind of printer's proof that reflects finished pages at low resolution. Used for final review of text, not art. Outside of the US, these proofs are often called Ozalids. Digital versions can be called e-blues or soft proofs.

blurb. A positive comment or review of a book that is used as part of its sales copy.

body text. The continuous, primary text in a book, in contrast to headings, captions, sidebars, etc. Also called running text.

body type. The typeface or font used for the **body text**.

book block. The bound pages of a book, the "inside" of a book.

book map. A page-by-page outline or snapshot of what should go where inside a book. Also called a flatplan.

bulk. The mass of a book based on its length, how "bulky" it is.

case. The hard cover of a hardcover book. *Or* the form of a letter: upper case, lower case, small caps. *Or* the relationship of uppercase and lowercase letters in a title, phrase, or passage: all caps, **title case, sentence case**.

case binding. Book construction in which pages are bound into a **case** and attached with **endpapers**. The most common method for binding **hardcover** books.

casewrap. The paper or cloth that covers the boards and spine of a book.

castoff. The roughest version of book's interior layout, used for estimating page and word-per-page count and other aspects of layout and sequencing.

chapter display. The information at the head of a chapter which may include the chapter number, chapter title, chapter subtitle, epigraph, or other introductory information.

character. A single letter, number, punctuation mark, or symbol within a **font**.

CMYK. The initialization for the inks used in **process color** printing: cyan, magenta, yellow, and black (*k* stands for the "key" color, which is black). CMYK is the mode required for images and files that will be *printed* in full color (as opposed to RGB, for red, green, and blue, which is the color mode used for display on screens).

color palette. The collection of colors used for a given design.

comps. Competitive or comparable books. Used to understand how a book fits into the landscape of other books of similar subject matter or genre. *Or* short for *comprehensive layout*, the stage between sketch and finished design.

creative brief. The document created to orient a designer (and the entire publishing team) to a book—usually includes a description, specs, relevant **comps**, and design direction.

crop marks. Short lines marking the corners of a page that indicate where the sheet will be trimmed in a finished book. Crop marks can also indicate where a piece of art should be **cropped**.

crop. To show a portion, rather than the entirety, of an image or other visual element.

dingbat. A typographic symbol or image that is included as a **character** in a **font**.

display type. Type that is used for titles and other headings, usually larger than **body type**.

double-page spread. Art that extends across both pages of a spread. Redundant but common lingo.

dummy. A blank version of a book produced to reflect its size, bulk, paper choice, and other **printer's specifications**, prior to printing.

dustjacket. See **jacket**.

ebook. A book presented in a digital format.

em. A unit of measurement that is relative to **point** size. For instance, in 12-point type the em is 12 points, and in 10-point type the em is 10 points.

endpaper. The sheet of paper at the front and back of a hardcover that attaches the **book block** to the **case**. Also called endsheet.

EPUB. The file format for reflowable **ebooks**. Short for electronic publication.

extent. See **page count**.

flatplan. See **book map**.

flyleaf. The half of the **endpaper** that isn't pasted down to the inside of the **case**.

F&Gs (folded and gathered signatures). The printed pages of a finished book before they're bound. Sometimes provided to publishers by the printer as a final check before binding.

folio. Another name for page number.

font. Historically, all the physical pieces that made up a specific typeface at a specific size. In the digital age, the file that tells a computer how to display a specific typeface. In common use, a set of characters bundled under a specific name (e.g., Times New Roman) and is interchangeable with **typeface**.

foredge. The edge of the book block opposite the spine edge.

format. The physical presentation of a book, primarily referring to its size and how it is bound. *See* **hardcover, paperback, mass-market paperback, ebook.**

FPO (for position only). Shorthand notation for a visual element being used as a placeholder, common in sample design or **galley** stages.

front matter. The portion of the book before the main body of the book. Commonly includes **half title, title page,** copyright information, dedication, epigraph, table of contents, preface, and foreword.

galleys. Used differently at different publishing houses, and sometimes not used at all. Commonly, refers to rounds of designed interior pages for review by authors and editors, e.g., first galleys, second galleys. These can also be called first pages, first proofs, first pass, or firsts.

grayscale. The color mode used when printing in one-color / black ink. Grayscale allows for a range of shades of black from 0 to 100 percent.

gutter. The inside margins of a **spread** that abut and fall into the book's **binding**.

half title. The first, **recto** page of a book, which (usually) displays the book's title and nothing else.

hardcover. Technically, a book whose covers are made of boards. In practice, the most expensive (to produce and to purchase) and prestigious publishing **format**.

head and tail bands. Decorative strips of cloth that are glued to the top and bottom of the **book block** in a **hardcover** book.

hinge. The area of the **case** between the spine and the front or back board that allows it to open and close. Used interchangeably with **joint**.

hyphen stack. A hyphen repeated at the end of two or more successive lines.

illustration. An umbrella term for the art (photographic, drawn, painted, collaged, or created digitally) inside a book. *Or* an image that is drawn, painted, or collaged, as opposed to a photograph. In the second context, can be referred to as an illo.

inset. Art or other visual elements that don't **bleed** off a page.

italic. A style of type in contrast to **roman**, or upright, type.

jacket. The removable paper wrapper that covers a **hardcover** case and contains the cover design and sales information about the book.

joint. The area of the **case** between the spine and the front or back board that allows them to open and close. Used interchangeably with **hinge**.

JPEG. A compressed file format for images that is appropriate for digital use. In general, images used for printed books should be converted from this file type to a noncompressed format such as **TIFF** or PSD.

justified. The alignment of text where both the left and right side of a line are flush to the margin, taking up the full **measure**. As opposed to **ragged** alignment.

kerning. The adjustment of space between any pair of **characters** sitting side by side.

leading. The vertical space between lines of type. Also called line spacing.

leaf. A sheet of paper inside a book. Each side of a leaf is a page.

letter spacing. See **tracking**.

line spacing. See **leading**.

margin. The space around the printed elements on a page. Includes upper, lower, inside, and outside margins.

mass-market paperback. An inexpensive paperback **format** (usually 4¼ × 7 inches), often sold in airports, grocery stores, drug stores, etc. in addition to bookstores.

mechanical. A final, print-ready design, e.g., the cover mechanical.

measure. The width of a **text block** or **text column**.

mood board. A physical or digital collection of visual ideas, generally gathered to explore the style or look of a cover or book interior.

orphan. The first line of a paragraph abandoned at the bottom of a page.

page count. The length of a book. Also called extent.

Pantone Matching System (PMS). The most commonly used ink system for **spot colors**.

paperback. Technically, a book whose cover is made of a single piece of stiff paper wrapped around front, back, and spine. In practice, the most common **format** for trade books.

part opener. The page or **spread** that introduces a major section, or part, of a book.

PDF (Portable Document Format). A platform-agnostic file format in which design is fixed but text is searchable and editable. Commonly used for sharing design at all stages, including final files to the printer.

perfect binding. Book construction in which a book's pages are bound with glue and the other three sides trimmed to create a neat or "perfect" edge. The most common method for binding **paperback** books.

pica. A unit of measurement in design and printing, for instance the page or **text column** size is often expressed in picas (inches, centimeters, and millimeters are also common). There are 12 **points** to a pica.

point. The most common unit of measurement for type, about $1/72$ of an inch. When speaking about a font, you refer to its point size.

print on demand (POD). The printing of a book only once it has been ordered, as opposed to a **print run** where copies are printed whether they have been ordered or not.

print run. The number of copies in a single printing of a book.

printer's specifications. All the details for how a book should be manufactured, including its size, length, binding type, how many colors to print, kind of papers and boards, additional effects, and any other information to produce a specific title. Also called production specifications, usually shortened to *specs*.

process color. Printing that creates color through a blend of **CMYK** inks. As opposed to **spot color**. Also called four color.

proofs. Digital or printed versions of covers, jackets, or book interiors intended to reflect the final printed version of same.

publisher's imprint. The logo, name, and location (city, state, or country) of the publisher. Placed in the lower portion of a **title page**.

pull quote. A typically short passage lifted from the primary text that is visually differentiated (usually presented larger or bolder) in order to highlight it.

ragged. (pronounced *rag-ed*) The alignment of text where the end of a line isn't flush to the margin. Can be ragged right (flush left) or, less often, ragged left (flush right). As opposed to **justified**.

reading line. A descriptive phrase that appears on a book's cover in addition to the title and subtitle.

recto. The right-hand page of a book **spread**. As opposed to **verso**.

resolution. The size and number of pixels that make up a digital image. Screen resolution is measured in pixels per inch (ppi) and print resolution is measured in dots per inch (dpi). High resolution, which is required for professional-quality printing, is 300 dpi at 100 percent size.

river. A noticeable pattern of white space running through the text block on a page.

roman. A style of type that developed in Italy in the late fifteenth century and came to be the most common style for typefaces created for the Latin alphabet. In popular use, refers to the upright form of a typeface, as opposed to **italic**.

rule. The term designers use for a vertical or horizontal line. (Dashes and hyphens aren't rules, they're **characters**.)

running head, running foot, running shoulder. Identifying text (often author name, book title, part or chapter title) repeated on most pages of the body of the book. Running heads appear in the top margin, running feet appear in the bottom margin, running shoulders appear in the outside margin.

running text. See **body text**.

runt line. See **widow**.

sales copy. Text intended for a back cover, or jacket flaps, that describes a book (flatteringly) to a potential reader.

sample design. The stage of interior design when type, layout, and style is first worked out using a representative portion of the text. Or the product of that effort.

sans serif. A typeface or individual **character** without **serifs**.

sentence case. The setting of a phrase or sentence in which the first letter of the phrase or sentence is capitalized, and all other characters are lower case, excepting proper nouns.

serif. As part of a letter, the line at the end of a stroke. As a category of type, a typeface or individual **character** with serifs.

short-run digital printing (SRDP). The name says it all: printing digitally, as opposed to printing offset, for short (or shortish) print runs—generally between ten and four thousand copies.

sidebar. A passage that is independent of, and visually differentiated from, the primary, or running, text.

signature. A gathering or "booklet" of pages created by a series of folds of a larger printed sheet. Books are made of multiple signatures that are sewn or glued together.

spot art. An **illustration** that isn't enclosed in a rectangle and has an organic edge.

spot color. Printing that creates color through the use of solid or single-color inks, often **Pantone** inks. Spot color is usually a more reliable representation of individual tones and can be used independently or in combination with **process color**.

spread. Two facing pages of a book.

tagging. The application of codes to the elements of a manuscript so their function can be understood by designers, and other humans, and computers. Also known as coding, styling, or markup.

text block. The primary section of text on a page. Some pages have multiple text blocks. Also called text column.

text column. See **text block**.

TIFF. A common uncompressed file format for images for use in printed books.

tint. A shade or percentage of a single color such as black or a **spot color**.

title case. The setting of a phrase or sentence in which most words are capitalized, usually excepting prepositions, some articles, and common coordinating conjunctions. Also called headline-style capitalization.

title page. The first full spread of a book, which displays the book's title, subtitle, author's name, other contributors, if appropriate, and the **publisher's imprint**.

TK. Publishing shorthand for content—written or visual—that is still "to come." (Yes, it's the wrong initials.)

tracking. Adding or subtracting space uniformly between the characters of a word, phrase, or passage. Words or phrases in all caps are usually tracked to create a little space between the characters. Also called letter spacing.

trim size. The size of the pages of a book. The boards of a hardcover will extend past the book block and be larger than the trim size.

typeface. A set of typographic characters sharing a style and bundled under a specific name (e.g., Times New Roman).

verso. The left-hand page of a book **spread**. As opposed to **recto**.

weight. How dark a typeface appears. For instance, thin, light, regular, book, bold, extra bold, heavy, and ultra are all possible references to a font's weight.

white line. A blank line within running text that serves as an editorial break.

widow. The last line of a paragraph that ends at the top of a page. *Or* the last word of a paragraph left alone on a line, also called a runt line.

word stack. An identical word (or words with identical roots) or phrase repeated at the beginning or end of two or more successive lines.

Notes

Chapter 1: The Physical Book

1. Roger Fawcett-Tang, *New Book Design* (London: Lawrence King, 2004), 11.

2. Tom Mole, *The Secret Life of Books: Why They Mean More Than Words* (London: Elliot & Thompson, 2019), 16.

3. Mole, *The Secret Life of Books*, 16.

4. In three-piece case construction, the spine is often covered with an additional piece of material, a classic look. The additional cloth was originally there as reinforcement, but when that was no longer necessary, the construction was kept as a design feature—it does look handsome and so much like a book! These days, the three-piece case effect is sometimes faked by *printing* the spine in a different color than the front and back covers—that is, it's not additional pieces of material, it's just meant to appear that way. No shade—I've employed this technique many times myself.

5. "Book Anatomy 101: Head and Tail Bands," Asia Pacific Offset, February 4, 2017, https://www.asiapacificoffset.com/blog_individual .aspx?bid=BLOG000084.

6. Publishing formats are important publishing strategies quite outside of any design implications. For more about the evolution of trade paperback and mass market formats and how they serve different ideas about readership, see John B. Thompson, *Book Wars: The Digital Revolution in Publishing* (Cambridge, UK: Polity Press, 2021), 48–52.

7. The idea of the unnecessary dominance of hardcovers comes from Brooke Warner, "What It Would Take to Disrupt the Publishing Industry," *Publishers Weekly*, October 8, 2021, https://www.publishersweekly.com/pw/by-topic /authors/pw-select/article/87575-what-it-would-take-to-disrupt-the -publishing-industry.html.

8. Michael Seidlinger, "Looking for Answers to Paper Shortages," *Publisher's Weekly*, February 24, 2022, https://www.publishersweekly.com/pw/by-topic /industry-news/manufacturing/article/88607-looking-for-answers-to-paper -shortages.html.

9. This was discussed as part of the panel "The New Future of Printing and Manufacturing" at the Publishing Professionals Network 2022 conference, Berkeley, CA, April 29, 2022.

10. Many US printers now exclusively use plant- and soy-based inks. Some printers also recycle their waste, run on renewable energy, and are conscious about the papers they source. The questions around sustainable chains of custody for paper and how credible are Forest Stewardship Council (FSC) and

Sustainable Forest Initiative (SFI) certifications are more complex than I can untangle. See the Twitter feed of @FSC-Watch for critique of the FSC and their own website for the other side of the argument (http://fsc.org). The website Recycled Paper Matters (http://recycledpapermatters.org) also discusses the arguments and has a list of North American paper manufacturers they consider the most environmentally responsible.

11. Thompson, *Book Wars*, 14–15.

Chapter 2: Type

1. The full quote is: "No one can say that the *o*'s roundness appeals to us only because it is like that of an apple or of a girl's breast or of the full moon. We like the circle because such liking is connatural to the human mind. . . . You don't draw an *A* and then stand back and say: there, that gives you a good idea of an *A* as seen through an autumn mist, or: that's not a real *A* but gives you a good effect of one. Letters are things, not pictures of things." Eric Gill, *Autobiography* (New York: Devin-Adair, 1941), 120.

2. Woodblock printing has been around since at least the sixth century in China, and printing with metal type was developed, again in China, in the eleventh century. The Chinese also invented paper. But the Latin alphabet, and its small character set, was more suited to the technology of casting type than the vast number of characters required for writing in Chinese, which helps explain its quick adaption in Europe. See S. H. Steinberg, *Five Hundred Years of Printing*, 3rd ed (Middlesex, England: Penguin Books, 1974), 23, and Robert Bringhurst, *The Elements of Typographic Style*, version 3.2. (Vancouver: Hartley & Marks, 2008), 119.

3. Tom Mole, *The Secret Life of Books*, 17.

4. S. H. Steinberg, *Five Hundred Years of Printing*, 25.

5. Warren Chappell and Robert Bringhurst, *A Short History of the Printed Word,* 2nd ed. (Vancouver: Hartley & Marks, 1999), 93.

6. Steinberg, *Five Hundred Years of Printing*, 27–28.

7. If you want to go deep on the history and evolution of type, there are some amazing books about typography out there. Check out "Further Readings" at the back of this book for some of my favorites.

8. Stephen Coles, *The Anatomy of Type* (New York: Harper Design, 2012) is a great reference for just this kind of detailed looking at letterforms.

9. See Gerard Unger, *While You're Reading* (New York: Mark Batty Publisher, 2007), 33 and 164, and Aries Arditi and Jianna Cho, "Serifs and Font Legibility," *Vision Research* 45, no. 23 (November 2005): 2926–33.

10. Paul McNeil, *The Visual History of Type* (London: Lawrence King, 2017), 347.

11. Michael Bierut, "Thirteen Ways of Looking at a Typeface," *Design Observer*, May 12, 2007, https://designobserver.com/feature/thirteen-ways-of-looking -at-a-typeface/5497.

12. Robert Bringhurst, *The Elements of Typographic Style* (Vancouver: Hartley & Marks, 2008), 53.

13. Bringhurst, *The Elements of Typographic Style*, 55.

14. McNeil, *The Visual History of Type*, 351.

15. Bringhurst, *The Elements of Typographic Style*, 22.

16. There is a fascinating exploration of this in Dave Addey, *Typeset in the Future* (New York: Abrams, 2018), 46–51.

17. Kaitlyn Tiffany, "This Font You Know from Old Pulp Novels Is All over New Books," *Vox*, January 17, 2019, https://www.vox.com /the-goods/2019/1/17/18185389/lydian-font-book-design-nancy-drew -against-everything.

18. Matthieu Lommen, ed., *The Book of Books: 500 Years of Graphic Innovation* (London: Thames and Hudson, 2012), 413.

Chapter 3: The Cover

1. Adam Gopnik, "How the Graphic Designer Milton Glaser Made America Cool Again," *New Yorker*, March 20, 2023.

2. Rodrigo Corral (@rodrigocorral_), "#RejectFriday from 2015. No matter how much experience you have, more work is rejected than approved in the publishing industry. It's a journey. Can't be a good cover, has to be the right cover," Instagram, July 9, 2021, https://www.instagram.com/p/CRHKSaSFYFy/.

3. The word *comp* is also short for *comprehensive layout*—a design that is further along than an initial sketch but not completely finished either.

4. Emily Temple, "The 17 Best Book Covers of May," *Literary Hub*, June 3, 2022, https://lithub.com/the-17-best-book-covers-of-may/.

5. See Eugenia Williamson, "Cover Girls: How Lipstick, Bathing Suits, and Naked Backs Discredit Women's Fiction," *Boston Globe*, June 28, 2014; and Anna Solomon, "Sexy Backs and Headless Women: A Book Cover Manifesto," *The Millions*, August 3, 2017, https://themillions.com/2017/08/tk-5.html.

6. Elliot Ross, "The Dangers of a Single Book Cover," *Africa Is a Country* (blog), May 7, 2014, https://africasacountry.com/2014/05/the-dangers-of-a-single -book-cover-the-acacia-tree-meme-and-african-literature/.

7. Michael Silverberg, "The Reason Every Book about Africa Has the Same Cover—and It's Not Pretty," *Quartz*, May 12, 2014, https://qz.com/207527 /the-reason-every-book-about-africa-has-the-same-cover-and-its-not-pretty/.

8. Peter Mendelsund, *Cover* (New York: PowerHouse, 2014), 162.

9. In many ways, this is not limited to cover design. John B. Thompson's *Book Wars: The Digital Revolution in Publishing* provides a comprehensive view of how Amazon has disrupted the publishing industry on many levels.

10. "Q & A with Isaac Tobin, University of Chicago Press," *The Casual Optimist* (blog), November 17, 2009, http://www.casualoptimist.com /blog/2009/11/17/q-a-with-isaac-tobin-university-of-chicago-press/.

11. Derek Birdsall, *Notes on Book Design* (New Haven: Yale University Press, 2004), 9.

Chapter 4: Inside the Book

1. Erin Somers, "Avid Reader Launches Credits Page Campaign," *Publisher's Lunch* (blog), May 3, 2023, https://lunch.publishersmarketplace.com/2023/05 /avid-reader-launches-credits-page-campaign/.

2. Chapter titles taken from Mark Argentsinger's *A Grammar of Typography: Classical Book Design in the Digital Age* (Boston: David R. Godine, 2020).

3. Edward R. Tufte, *Envisioning Information* (Cheshire, CT: Graphics Press, 1990), 34.

4. Hans Peter Willberg and Friedrich Forssman, *Lesetypografie* (Mainz: Hermann Schmidt, 1997), quoted in Gerard Unger, *While You're Reading* (New York: Mark Batty, 2007), 22.

5. The idea of the tempo of line lengths comes from Cyrus Highsmith in his book *Inside Paragraphs: Typographic Fundamentals* (Hudson, NY: Princeton Architectural Press, 2020), 83–85.

6. Robert Bringhurst, *The Elements of Typographic Style*, 26.

7. Or maybe it's the reverse. A review of the literature reveals a variety of contradictory opinions on which scenario is a widow and which an orphan. To complicate matters further, runt lines are also sometimes referred to as widows.

Chapter 5: Illustrated Books

1. Whether images should be placed symmetrically or asymmetrically on a page was once a question that riveted the design world. If you're interested in more context, look up Jan Tschichold in any graphic design survey.

2. Although there is an argument to be made for density. Discussing the thinking of the information designer Edward Tufte, Ellen Lupton argues for the benefits of information-rich pages: "In order to help readers make connections and comparisons as well as to find information quickly, a single surface packed with well-organized information is sometimes better than multiple

pages with lots of blank space. In typography as in urban life, density invites intimate exchange among people and ideas." Ellen Lupton, *Thinking with Type: A Critical Guide for Designers, Writers, Editors, and Students* (New York: Princeton Architectural Press, 2004), 75.

Chapter 6: Ebooks

1. James Hardy, "A History of Ebooks," *History Cooperative*, September 15, 2016, https://historycooperative.org/the-history-of-e-books/.

2. These figures are from 2018 and come from Thompson, *Book Wars*, 29. This is assymetrically distributed over genre with ebooks accounting for over 50 percent of romance titles, while probably much less than 15 percent of categories like travel, cookbooks, and kids' books (*Book Wars*, 39 and 46).

3. "In a 2018 survey of 500 Canadian readers of digital books, 45% were ebooks, 43% were print, and 12% were audiobooks. Ebook readers do still read a lot of print, as some genres cater more to the digital format than others. . . . For example, 44% of digital readers prefer to read cookbooks in print vs. 17% in digital format. Upshot: Many digital readers read in both formats." Kira Harkonen, "Who Is the Average Ebook Reader?" *BookNet Canada*, July 17, 2018, https://www.booknetcanada.ca/blog/2018/7/17/who-is-the-average-ebook-reader.

4. Mike Shatzkin and Robert Paris Riger, *The Book Business: What Everyone Needs to Know* (Oxford: Oxford University Press, 2019), 60.

5. Shatzkin and Riger, *The Book Business*, 62. The pricing of ebooks has been a publishing drama. Shatzkin and Riger give a summary of the key dynamics, and Thompson's *Book Wars* has a play-by-play in chapter 5.

6. Thompson, *Book Wars*, 416.

7. Thompson, *Book Wars*, chap. 5.

8. "Amazon: Reinventing the Book," *Newsweek*, November 17, 2007.

9. Thompson, *Book Wars*, 49–50.

10. Stephen Fry (@stephenfry), "This is the point. One technology doesn't replace another, it complements. Books are no more threatened by Kindle than stairs by elevators," Twitter, March 11, 2009, 2:07 p.m., https://twitter.com/stephenfry/status/1312682218.

11. Monica Anderson, "The Demographics of Device Ownership," Pew Research Center, October 29, 2015, https://www.pewresearch.org/internet/2015/10/29/the-demographics-of-device-ownership/.

12. Thompson, *Book Wars*, 39.

13. John Brownlee, "The Kindle Finally Gets Typography That Doesn't Suck," *Fast Company*, May 27, 2015, https://www.fastcompany.com/3046678 /the-kindle-finally-gets-typography-that-doesnt-suck.

14. Khoi Vinh, "Control" (slide presentation and live talk, AIGA Next, Denver, October 13, 2007).

15. This networking and nesting of information was part of the earliest visions of how digital books could reinvent how reading might work. In the 1990s, some authors played with hyperlinks as a narrative device, allowing users to choose and help create the story they were reading, stretching the idea of what a novel could be. The novel *afternoon, a story* (all lowercase), published in 1990 by the author Michael Joyce, and *Patchwork Girl* by Shelly Jackson, published in 1995, are considered pioneering works of hypertext narrative.

16. Ellen Lupton, ed., *Type on Screen: A Critical Guide for Designers, Writers, Developers, and Students* (New York: Princeton Architectural Press, 2014), 71.

17. David Cramer, "The Past, Present, and Future of Digital Publishing That Hasn't, Isn't, but May Still Meet the Promise of the Web" (presentation, Ebookcraft 2019, Toronto, March 19, 2019).

18. Shatzkin and Riger, *The Book Business*, 58.

19. Tom Corson-Knowles, "List of the Top #100 Most Competitive Amazon Kindle Bestseller Categories 2021," TCK Publishing, accessed February 28, 2022, https://www.tckpublishing.com/competitive-amazon-kindle -bestseller-categories/.

20. "99%+ of the ebooks created commercially are reflowable." David Kudler, "Going against the Flow: Reflowable vs. Fixed-Layout Ebooks," *The Book Designer* (blog), September 21, 2020, https://www.thebookdesigner.com /going-against-the-flow-reflowable-vs-fixed-layout-ebooks/.

21. Thompson, *Book Wars*, 46.

22. Lincoln Michel, "Maybe the Book Doesn't Need to Be 'Disrupted' in the First Place?" *CounterCraft* (blog), January 24, 2023, https://countercraft.substack .com/p/maybe-thebook-doesnt-need-to-disrupted.

23. I needed (and found) a lot of help when writing this chapter, including from the following sources: Charles Nix, "A Typographic Methodology for Ebooks" (presentation, Ebookcraft 2014, Toronto, March 5, 2014); David Cramer, "The Past, Present, and Future of Digital Publishing That Hasn't, Isn't, but May Still Meet the Promise of the Web"; Monique Mongeon and Noah Genner, "How We Read Digitally" (presentation, Ebookcraft 2018, Toronto, March 22, 2018); Greg Albers, "Closer to Metal" (presentation, Ebookcraft 2016, Toronto, March 31, 2016); Iris Amelia Febres, "The Art of Storyboarding" (presenta- tion, Ebookcraft 2016, Toronto, March 31, 2016); Anne-Marie Concepción, "InDesign CC to Epub" (LinkedIn Learning webinar, June 26, 2018) and

"Ebook Foundations" (LinkedIn Learning webinar, September 18, 2017); Nigel French, "InDesign CC EPUB Typography" (LinkedIn Learning webinar, July 30, 2015).

Chapter 7: The Design Process

1. Jhumpa Lahiri writes movingly about reacting to her book's covers in *The Clothing of Books* (New York: Vintage, 2016), where some of these ideas come from. The quote is from page 18.

2. "Ten Rules for Writing Fiction," *Guardian*, February 20, 2010, https://www.theguardian.com/books/2010/feb/20/ten-rules-for-writing-fiction-part-one.

3. Peter Mendelsund, *Cover* (New York: PowerHouse, 2014), 131.

4. There are a variety of methods for markup. It can be as simple as applying styles within Word or other word processing software. Some publishers use visible tags within their manuscripts in which the tags themselves can be read (and must be deleted) by a designer, for instance, <i>italicize this phrase</i>. Many publishers have moved to an XML workflow that facilitates correct and thorough coding from the editor's desk through design and ebook conversion. Some writers, editors, and copyeditors are intimidated by the mechanics of tagging, but it's a basic part of preparing a manuscript in the digital age. More information about markup can be found in *CMOS* 17, 2.81–83.

5. There are two kinds of color proofs: There are "wet proofs" in which a portion of a book is run on a press using the same process that will be used for the actual printing, with the same inks and same paper that will be used in the eventual book. These are costly and it's a rare publisher who will shell out for them. Digital proofs, sometimes called Epson proofs, are faster, cheaper, and more readily available. Although they use a different printing process—inkjet versus offset printing—and different paper, they're calibrated to represent the reproduction of color in a final printing situation. These are certainly better than nothing but are still only an approximation of the final result.

Appendix

1. Robin Williams, *The Non-Designer's Type Book: Insights and Techniques for Creating Professional-Level Type* (Berkeley, CA: Peachpit Press, 1998), 146.

Further Readings

As much as I've said here, there is *a lot* that has gone unsaid regarding design, typography, printing, and publishing. If you are inspired to learn more, there are so many amazing books on these subjects. Here are the ones that have informed and inspired me over my career and while writing this book.

Book Design

Argetsinger, Mark. *A Grammar of Typography: Classical Book Design in the Digital Age*. Boston: David R. Godine, 2020.

Bartram, Alan. *Five Hundred Years of Book Design*. New Haven: Yale University Press, 2001.

Birdsall, Derek. *Notes on Book Design*. New Haven: Yale University Press, 2004.

Bringhurst, Robert. *The Surface of Meaning: Books and Book Design in Canada*. Vancouver, BC: CCSP Press, 2008.

De Bondt, Sara, and Fraser Muggeridge, eds., *The Form of the Book Book*. London: Occasional Papers, 2020.

Dwiggins, W. A. *Layout in Advertising*. Rev. ed. New York: Harper and Brothers, 1948.

Hendel, Richard. *On Book Design*. New Haven: Yale University Press, 1998.

Hendel, Richard, ed. *Aspects of Contemporary Book Design*. Iowa City: University of Iowa Press, 2013.

Hochuli, Jost, and Robin Kinross. *Designing Books: Practice and Theory*. London: Hyphen Press, 1996.

Lommen, Mathieu, ed. *The Book of Books: 500 Years of Graphic Innovation*. London: Thames and Hudson, 2012.

Mitchell, Michael, and Susan Wightman. *Book Typography: A Designer's Manual*. Marlborough, UK: Libanus Press, 2005.

Tschihold, Jan. *The Form of the Book: Essays on the Morality of Good Design*. Translated by Hajo Hadeler. Vancouver: Hartley & Marks, 1991.

Books and Reading

Bringhurst, Robert. *What Is Reading For?* Rochester, NY: RIT Cary Graphic Arts Press, 2011.

Duncan, Dennis. *Index, A History of The: A Bookish Adventure from Medieval Manuscripts to the Digital Age*. New York: W. W. Norton, 2022.

Houston, Keith, *The Book: A Cover-to-Cover Exploration of the Most Powerful Object of Our Time*. New York: W. W. Norton, 2016.

Mole, Tom. *The Secret Life of Books: Why They Mean More Than Words*. London: Elliot & Thompson, 2019.

Unger, Gerard. *While You're Reading*. New York: Mark Batty, 2007.

Cover Design

Bache, Stuart. *The Author's Guide to Cover Design*. Shrewsbury, UK: Books Covered, 2018.

Drew, Ned, and Paul Sternberger. *By Its Cover: Modern American Book Cover Design*. New York: Princeton Architectural Press, 2005.

Fawcett-Tang, Roger, ed. *New Book Design*. London: Lawrence King, 2004.

Kidd, Chip. *Book One: Work: 1986–2006*. New York: Rizzoli, 2005.

Lahiri, Jhumpa. *The Clothing of Books*. New York: Vintage, 2016.

Mendelsund, Peter. *Cover*. New York: PowerHouse, 2014.

Mendelsund, Peter, and David J. Alworth. *The Look of the Book: Jackets, Covers, and Art at the Edges of Literature*. California: Ten Speed Press, 2020.

Power, Alan. *Front Cover: Great Book Jackets and Cover Design*. London: Mitchell Beazley, 2001.

Graphic Design

Bierut, Michael. *Seventy-Nine Short Essays on Design*. New York: Princeton Architectural Press, 2007.

Eskilson, Stephen J. *Graphic Design: A New History*. New Haven: Yale University Press, 2007.

Kennett, Bruce. *W. A. Dwiggins: A Life in Design*. San Francisco: Letterform Archive, 2017.

Lupton, Ellen, Farrah Kafei, Jennifer Tobias, Josh A. Halstead, Kaleena Sales, Leslie Xia, and Valentina Vergara. *Extra Bold*. New York: Princeton Architectural Press, 2021.

Meggs, Philip B. *A History of Graphic Design*. New York: Wiley, 1998.

Millman, Debbie. *The Essential Principles of Graphic Design*. Cincinnati: How Books, 2008.

Siegler, Bonnie. *Dear Client, This Book Will Teach You How to Get What You Want from Creative People*. New York: Artisan, 2018.

Tufte, Edward R. *Envisioning Information*. Cheshire, CT: Graphics Press, 1990.

Production

Pocket Pal: A Graphic Arts Production Handbook. 21st ed. Memphis: International Paper Company, 2019.

Publishing and Self-Publishing

Friedman, Jane. *The Business of Being a Writer*. Chicago: University of Chicago Press, 2018.

Ginna, Peter, ed. *What Editors Do: The Art, Craft, and Business of Book Editing*. Chicago: University of Chicago Press, 2017.

Maum, Courtney. *Before and after the Book Deal: A Writer's Guide to Finishing, Publishing, Promoting, and Surviving Your First Book*. New York: Catapult, 2020.

Penn, Joanna. *Successful Self-Publishing: How to Self-Publish and Market Your Book*. Curl Up Press, 2021.

Ronn, M. L. *150 Self-Publishing Questions Answered: Alli's Writing, Publishing, and Book Marketing Tips for Indie Authors and Poets*. Font, 2020.

Saller, Carol Fisher. *The Subversive Copy Editor: Advice from Chicago (or, How to Negotiate Good Relationships with Your Writers, Your Colleagues, and Yourself)*. 2nd ed. Chicago: University of Chicago Press, 2016.

Shatzkin, Mike, and Robert Paris Riger. *The Book Business: What Everyone Needs to Know*. Oxford: Oxford University Press, 2019.

Thompson, John B. *Book Wars: The Digital Revolution in Publishing*. Cambridge, UK: Polity Press, 2021.

Trubek, Anne. *So You Want to Publish a Book?* Cleveland: Belt, 2020.

Warner, Brooke. *Green-Light Your Book: How Writers Can Succeed in the New Era of Publishing*. Berkeley, CA: She Writes Press, 2016.

Style Guides

The Chicago Manual of Style. 17th ed. Chicago: University of Chicago Press, 2017.

Strunk, William, Jr., and E. B. White. *The Elements of Style*. 2nd ed. New York: Macmillan, 1972.

Typography

Addey, Dave. *Typeset in the Future*. New York: Abrams, 2018.

Bringhurst, Robert. *The Elements of Typographic Style*. Version 3.2. Vancouver: Hartley & Marks, 2008.

Bringhurst, Robert. *Palatino: The Natural History of a Typeface*. Boston: David R. Godine, 2016.

Butterick, Matthew. *Typography for Lawyers: Essential Tools for Polished and Persuasive Documents*. 2nd ed. Houston: O'Connor's, 2015.

Catich, Edward M. *The Origin of the Serif*. 2nd ed. Edited by Mary W. Gilroy. Davenport, Iowa: The Catich Gallery, St. Ambrose University, 1991.

Chappell, Warren, and Robert Bringhurst. *A Short History of the Printed Word*. 2nd ed. Vancouver: Hartley & Marks, 1999.

Coles, Stephen. *The Anatomy of Type*. New York: Harper Design, 2012.

Davies, Anna. *Glyph: A Visual Exploration of Punctuation Marks and Other Typographic Symbols*. London: Cicado Books, 2015.

Felici, James. *The Complete Manual of Typography: A Guide to Setting Perfect Type*. Berkeley, CA: Peachpit Press, 2003.

Gill, Eric. *An Essay on Typography*. London: Penguin Classics, 2013.

Highsmith, Cyrus. *Inside Paragraphs: Typographic Fundamentals*. Hudson, NY: Princeton Architectural Press, 2020.

Hochuli, Jost. *Detail in Typography: Letters, Letterspacing, Words, Wordspacing, Lines, Linespacing, Columns*. London: Hyphen Press, 2008.

Kane, John. *A Type Primer*. 2nd ed. London: Laurence King, 2011.

Lawson, Alexander. *Anatomy of a Typeface*. Boston: David R. Godine, 1990.

Lupton, Ellen. *Thinking with Type: A Critical Guide for Designers, Writers, Editors, and Students*. New York: Princeton Architectural Press, 2004.

Lupton, Ellen, ed. *Type on Screen: A Critical Guide for Designers, Writers, Developers, and Students*. New York: Princeton Architectural Press, 2014.

McNeil, Paul. *The Visual History of Type*. London: Lawrence King, 2017.

Morison, Stanley. *First Principles of Typography*. Cambridge: The University Press, 1951.

One Hundred Books Famous in Typography. New York: The Grolier Club, 2021.

Spiekermann, Erik, and E. M. Ginger. *Stop Stealing Sheep and Find Out How Type Works*. Berkeley, CA: Adobe Press, 2003.

Steinberg, S. H. *Five Hundred Years of Printing*. 3rd ed. London: Penguin, 1974.

Tracy, Walter. *Letters of Credit: A View of Type Design*. Jaffrey, NH: David R. Godine, 1986.

Waller, Robert H. W. "Graphic Aspects of Complex Texts: Typography as Macropunctuation." In *Processing of Visible Language*, ed. Paul A. Kolers, Merald E. Wrolstad, and Herman Bouma. Boston: Springer, 1980.

Warde, Beatrice. *The Crystal Goblet: Sixteen Essays on Typography*. London: Sylvan Press, 1955.

Williams, Jim. *Type Matters*. London: Merrell, 2012.

Williams, Robin. *The Mac Is Not a Typewriter*. 2nd ed. Berkeley, CA: Peachpit Press, 2003.

Image Credits

Illustrations on all chapter openers as well as pages 12, 17, 20, 34, 102, and 121 by Vivian Barad.

Page 36 Blackletter Print of 1476 of Pliny the Elder in Italian, printer: Jenson. Atalanta, CC BY-SA 3.0 via Wikimedia Commons.

Page 36 Roman type, Atalanta, CC BY-SA 3.0 via Wikimedia Commons.

Page 52 *The Bungalow Mystery* by Carolyn Keene. Cover designer unknown.

Page 52 *First Person* by Richard Flanagan. Cover design by Carole Devine Carson.

Page 71 *The Tipping Point* by Malcolm Gladwell. Cover design by Michael Ian Kaye.

Page 71 *Build* by Tony Faddell. Copyright © 2022 by Tony Faddell. Used by permission of HarperCollins Publishers. Cover design by Matteo Vianello.

Page 71 *Sapiens* by Yuval Noah Harari. Copyright © 2015 by Yuval Noah Harari. Used by permission of HarperCollins Publishers. Cover design by Suzanne Dean.

Page 73 *Portnoy's Complaint* by Philip Roth. Cover design by Paul Bacon.

Page 73 *Bonfire of the Vanities* by Tom Wolfe. Cover design by Fred Marcellino.

Page 73 *The Vanishing Half* by Brit Bennet. Cover design by Lauren Peters-Collaer.

Page 76 *City of Bones* by Cassandra Clare, copyright © 2007 Cassandra Claire, LLC. Reprinted with the permission of Margaret K. McElderry Books, an imprint of Simon & Schuster Children's Publishing Division. All rights reserved. Cover designer unknown.

Page 76 *1st to Die* by James Patterson, copyright © 2000. Reprinted by permission of Little Brown, an imprint of Hachette Book Group, Inc. Cover designer unknown.

Page 76 *Six Degrees of Scandal* by Caroline Linden. Copyright © 2016 by P. F. Belsley. Used by permission of HarperCollins Publishers. Cover designer unknown.

Page 76 *The Girl with the Dragon Tattoo* by Stieg Larsson. Cover design by Peter Mendelsund.

Page 76 *Fifty Shades of Grey* by E. L. James. Cover design by Jennifer McGuire.

Page 76 *Twilight* by Stephenie Meyer. Cover design by Gail Doobinin.

Page 77 *How the Word Is Passed* by Clint Smith. Cover design by Lucy Kim.

Page 77 *Thick* by Tressie McMillan Cottom. Cover design by Oliver Munday.

Page 77 *Swing Time* by Zadie Smith. Cover design by Jon Gray/gray318.

Page 78 *200 Women* copyright © Sharon Gelman, Marianne Lassandro, Geoff Blackwell, Ruth Hobday, eds. Photographs by Kieran Scott. Used with permission of Chronicle Books, LLC. Cover design by Alice Chau.

Page 78 *Black Food* by Bryant Terry. Cover design by George McCalman.

Page 78 *The Love and Lemons Cookbook* by Jeanine Donofrio. Cover design by Trina Bentley.

Page 85 *Everything Is Illuminated* by Jonathan Safran Foer. Copyright © 2002 by Jonathan Safran Foer. Used by permission of HarperCollins Publishers. Cover design by Jon Gray/gray318.

Pages 88, 95 Banjo, Yucalora/Shutterstock.

Page 140 Book map from *Drawn on the Way: A Guide to Capturing the Moment through Live Sketching* by Sarah Nisbett, published by Quarry Books.

Page 142 A page from *Feed Your People* by Leslie Jonath.

Page 143 Bulldog, Eric Isselee/Shutterstock.

Pages 143, 144 *Mona Lisa*, Bridgeman Images.

Acknowledgments

Thanks to:

Vivian Barad, whose illustrations bring so much delight to this book;

Jennifer Berne, my first and best reader;

Leslie Jonath, who believed from the beginning and helped me figure out the title;

Chicory Ruyle, who nailed the subtitle;

Frances Baca, who read a draft of the manuscript and provided essential insights and corrections;

John D. Berry, who provided expert, late-game counsel;

the publishing professionals who helped me think through the issues in this book: Amy Armstrong, Jerry Brennan, Andrea Burnett, Jennifer Conn, Maureen Forys, Beth Frankl, Jane Friedman, Regina Grenier, Richard Hendel, Mike Johnson, Kaitlin Ketchum, Adrianna Sutton, Gita Manaktala, Jess Morphew, Kara Plikaitis, Rachel Neumann, Susan Rabiner, Leigh Saffold, Linda Secondari, Dana Sloan, Danielle Svetcov, Kristen Tate, Rachel Toor, Jessica Walker, Brooke Warner, and Beth Wright;

the authors who shared their experiences with me: Louis Bayard, Emma Bernay, Kateri Ewing, Aaron Hamburger, Avner Landes, Hilary Leichter, Mike Mechanic, Patrick Roberts, and Philip Dean Walker;

the digital readers who helped me understand the appeal: Leo Jacoby, Kimberly Shirai, and Jenny Lefcourt (who also proffered the most beautiful place on earth for me to write on many occasions);

and the folks at the University of Chicago Press: my editor, Mary Laur, who was interested in my proposal from a blind email (miracle!) and whose editorial mastery and support has given me confidence throughout the process and made this book a reality; design director extraordinaire Jill Shimabukuro; ebook guru Denise Kennedy; assistant editor Mollie McFee and editorial associate Andrea Blatz; senior production editor Tamara Ghattas; editorial assistants Lily Sadowsky and McKenna Smith; student assistant Vichar Lochan; promotions manager Adrienne Meyers; and associate marketing director Jenny Ringblom; as well as freelancers copyeditor Trevor Perri; proofreader Mikayla Butchart; and indexer Theresa Wolner;

my mom and dad, whose attention and interest has always shone down on me like sunshine, and who passed along the writing genes;

and Dave and Mingus, who let me go away to write with smiles on their faces and put up with so much typography talk at the dinner table—you are the loves of my life.

Index

Page numbers in italics refer to figures.

traditional publishing: design team, 168–72; design process, 168–85; and ebooks, 154

trim sizes, 21–22, 28, 116, 122, 181, 208, 210; and covers, 67, 79; defined, 225; and illustrated books, 137; of mass-market paperbacks, 20; and printer specs, 18; as printing consideration, 25; small, 20

Tschichold, Jan, 229n1

Tufte, Edward, 116–17, 229n2, 229n3

type, 30–57, 227–28nn1–18; as art form, 35; blackletter, 35, 36, 38, 43, 44; and characters, 45–49; choosing, 49–55; and covers, 54, 82–84, 83–84, 87–88, 88; digital, 36, 52, 158–60; etiquette, 204–7, 232n1; and familiarity, 53; and fashion, 52–53; and functionality, 50; history, evolution, origins of, 33–36, 36, 51, 227n7; and illustrated books, 144, 145–46; and images, 87–88, 88, 144; and letters, 32, 35, 37; metal, 34, 43, 45, 55, 227n2; and punctuation, 47–48, 105; resources, 232n1, 235–36; sizes, 23, 55–56, 56, 108, 163; styling, 56–57, 57, 113, 146; and symbols, 48; text *versus* display, 44; and tone, 51. *See also* body type; characters; fonts; hierarchy; letters; typefaces; typesetting; typography

typefaces: boring, 44; and characters, 48; choosing, 49–55, 57; and covers, 82–84, 83–84, 92, 94; defined, 225; and ebooks, 53–54, 158–60; and familiarity with, 53; and fashion, 52–53; vs. fonts, 43; and letters, 37; and non-English words, 45; and punctuation, 47; and scripts, 42; and spines, 94; and styling, 56–57, 57, 113, 146; for titles, 83, 191; weight of, 225. *See also* body type; fonts; type; typography

typesetting, 39, 46, 53, 123–30, 179, 182–83; and alignment, 126–27; and compositors, 172; and corrections, 182; digital, 123; and ebooks, 158; etiquette, 204; and style guides, 181. *See also* hierarchy; type

typography: for cover design, 82–84, 83–84, 87–88, 88; and density, 229–30n2; and design, 32–57, 197; and ebooks, 53–54, 152, 158–60, 159, 164; and editing, 204; and hand lettering, 84–85; and hierarchy, 81–82, 113; and illustrated books, 145–46, 146; resources, 235–36; and space, 81–82, 100, 164; on spines, 94–95. *See also* fonts; type; typefaces; typesetting

underlining, 129, 197, 198

verso, 100–101, 104, 108, 223; blank, 101; defined, 225. *See also* rectos; spreads

Vignelli, Massimo, 53

visual books. *See* illustrated books

warehousing: costs of, 27–28; and team effort in publishing, 108

Warner, Brooke, 226n7

weight: of boards, 25; of books, 9; defined, 225; of dummies, 184; of ebooks, 8, 155, 160; of fonts/type, 56, 225; and hierarchy, 81; and images in ebooks, 160; of paper, 24, 183; and signatures, 23

white lines, as editorial breaks, defined, 225

white space. *See* negative space; space

widows: defined, 129, 225; and orphans, 129–30, 157, 181, 196–97, 229n7; and runt lines, 129–30, 197, 225, 229n7

wire-o format, 20, 20

word stacks: avoiding, 129; defined, 225

writers. *See* authors

XML, for markup and tagging, 180, 193, 232n4

YA (young adult) fiction, covers and jackets for, 12–13, 75–76, 86, 216

 **Chicago Guides to Writing, Editing, and Publishing**

A complete list of series titles is available on the
University of Chicago Press website.

About the Type

This book is set in three typefaces.

The body text is in Dolly Pro, a font family created by the type foundry Underware in 2001. The letters are strong and solid but the effect is warm and easygoing. Because it's low contrast—that is, the strokes never get too fine or too thick—it reads well as body text. And the italic is so pretty. I love how it dances on the line.

The chapter openers and primary headings are in Larsseit, a typeface created by the type designer Nico Inosanto in 2013. This sans serif appeals for the same reasons as Dolly—it combines easy readability, open letterforms, and low-contrast strokes with a good-natured vibe. It is clean but quirky (I love its lowercase g), both friendy *and* cool, which is a nice match with the voice I am trying to capture (in this book and in my life).

I wanted something efficient and versatile for captions and other text-sized sans serif and turned to the workhorse Whitney. This typeface was originally designed in 1996 for the Whitney Museum in New York by Tobias Frere-Jones. Whitney has many moods—its thinnest profile used in all uppercase is very chic; the medium and semibold faces are black enough to announce themselves but are not overly chunky. Because of its flexibility, dependability, and snappy style I have used Whitney in dozens of books over the years.